C000005289

When Spirit & Word Collide

The prophesied new wave of extraordinary churches

JARROD COOPER

RIVER
PUBLISHING

River Publishing & Media Ltd
Barham Court
Teston
Maidstone
Kent
ME18 5BZ
United Kingdom

info@river-publishing.co.uk

ISBN 978-1-908393-52-4
Cover design by www.spiffingcovers.com
Printed in the United Kingdom by Bell and Bain Ltd, Glasgow

Contents

What Others Are Saying...

"This is a timely, highly valuable book addressing one of the most important issues facing churches in the UK today. Jarrod skillfully grapples with how, as a church pastor, he can give appropriate attention to honouring the Word and the Spirit. With humility and honesty he opens a discussion that ought to challenge all of us. Are we passionate for God to move powerfully in our land again? If we are, we will need to be 'people of the Word' and 'people of the Spirit.'"
Stuart Bell, Senior leader of Alive Church and Leader of the Ground Level Network

"Jarrod Cooper is not just writing this excellent book from a theoretical point of view – he lives out experientially the principles contained within. The call today for Christians everywhere to be both people of God's Word and of God's Spirit has never been more needed. I am delighted to recommend this significant publication to you."
John Partington, National Leader of Assemblies of God Great Britain

"For those who have a desire to experience the presence and power of the Holy Spirit, and at the same time be part of the plan of God for His glorious Church, this book is most definitely for you. The Church of Jesus Christ is at a crossroads right now, with many voices expressing what direction we must take. I recommend that we hear Jarrod Cooper's voice in the pages of this book and heed the sentiments he has so powerfully expressed. It is the Word

and Spirit working together that will build the Church, penetrate darkness, establish the kingdom of God and transform nations in this crucial hour."
Ken Gott, Apostolic Leader, Bethshan Church and the House of Prayer, Europe

"Jarrod has taken Smith Wigglesworth's well known prophetic words and has examined and challenged the Church in our nation both historically and presently. I believe that the comparisons he brings about the condition of both Church and society are vital reading for today's Church leaders. I will be giving a copy to all my staff!"
Rt Rev'd David E Carr OSL, Order and Community of St Leonard

"Should your heart have a deep longing for an unprecedented move of God within your nation and beyond, then this is a must read book for you today."
David L'Herroux, UCB Chief Executive

"This excellent book focuses (or refocuses) our attention on God's intentions for His Church. Packed with insights, Scriptures and some great quotable quotes it is a must read."
Gerald Coates, Author, broadcaster, pioneer

"Finally! Somebody has said it! My heart was stirred as I read the words of *When Spirit and Word Collide*. It is an insightful and timely message for the Church! Jarrod finds a language for what 'those who have an ear to hear' are about to experience in their churches and ministries. I too believe that there is a definite shift occurring in God's great Church: a coming together, a collision of both the Word and the Spirit; it's already happening in seed form.

Jesus was masterful at moving in both realms seamlessly. He preached His Word with authority and then demonstrated its power with signs and wonders following. The people came from miles around to hear His Word and to be healed and made free! O that they might just touch the hem of His garment...

God is raising up a new order, friend. Jarrod beautifully explains in this wonderful book that we will be seeing much more of these kind of churches in the times to come, as men and women from both sides of the equation 'unify' and run together for the greatest move of God that the UK and beyond has ever seen. A must read!"
Mark Stevens, Worship leader

"*When Spirit and Word Collide* is an outstanding interpretation of what God is saying to pastors and church leaders in this 21st Century! Jarrod Cooper is a young apostolic leader with an uncanny insight on how to lead and grow a church that has a balance between powerful preaching, prophetic utterance, signs and wonders, a strong presence of God, and yet remains organised, vision-driven and systematic.

This book is a must read for every lead pastor and church leader, not only in the UK and Europe, but in the United States and the English speaking world. It is a dynamic interpretation and 'how to' application of Smith Wigglesworth's extraordinary 1947 prophecy about the latter years of the Church. It is a call not only to pray for

revival, but how to prepare for revival."
David Garcia, Lead Pastor, Grace World Outreach Church Brooksville, Florida, USA

"The moment I read the title of this book, I had a witness that this was a timely book from the heart of a hearer. You may ask why? The answer is easy: because that is what happened in my family. They were strong Word people when the Spirit and Word collided, which has resulted in a continuing response to the Great Commission. In this book Jarrod has captured the rhythm of heaven like a songwriter who is able to pen lyrics that lead you into the presence of God. It will lead you to ask: If not now, when, and if not us, who?"
Cleddie Keith, Senior Pastor, Heritage Fellowship, Florence, USA

"There are signs today in the Western Church of a holy dissatisfaction with the status quo of 'business as usual' in churches and ministries. There is a fresh hunger for another wave of the presence and power of God to revive the Church and awaken the world to the reality of the living, miracle-working Christ. In his latest book, Jarrod draws upon Scripture, Smith Wigglesworth's now famous 'Spirit and Word' prophecy, and a great wealth of personal experience to stir our hearts to a renewed pursuit of God; one that will lead first to personal transformation, then to church and community transformation, and ultimately to the fulfilment of God's great promises to fill the earth with the experiential knowledge of His glory!

Full of insight, godly provocation and biblical wisdom, I

highly commend *When Spirit and Word Collide* to you. May it provoke you, as it has me, to a renewed encounter with our wonder-working God, and an insatiable hunger for authentic Holy Spirit power in the Church of Jesus Christ.
Jonathan Conrathe, Founder Mission24

"I know Jarrod Cooper to be a man who not only loves revival, but who loves the Reviver Himself. The revelation presented in this book is a clarion call to the Church at large. God is getting ready to pour out His Spirit in an unprecedented way, and we must let 'the Spirit and the Word collide' if we are to experience His fullness. Well done, Jarrod!"
Lydia Stanley Marrow, Worship leader, Shake The Nations

"As I opened this book, my spirit began to dance. Jarrod had put into words the expectations of my spirit, being a revivalist in a generation that seems unaware that its mandate is to live out the prophetic move of God in this season. This book brings and ties us to the current prophetic trends of our generation and releases a revelation of heaven on earth through the Church!"
Noel Robinson, Worship Leader

"*When Spirit and Word Collide* is like reading a journal of personal discovery. I first met Jarrod in 1993 and was immediately drawn to a young man whose heartbeat was the same as mine. A heart for the kingdom, power and glory – and, as a result, to see people supernaturaly transformed into the very image of Christ. As you read you will be tracking his encounters with Jesus Christ, his quest for revival, his revelation of the Word, his insight into the Spirit, his love for the Bride, and his understanding of how the seemingly mundane and practical impact and enhance the 'spiritual'.

We are on a collision course with a revival of epic proportions. Ignore or embrace; prepare or postpone; on the fringes or in the fire; permanent or passing results. These are some of the choices we have. Read and apply. Here it comes: a collision!"

John Wasserman, Airport Christian Fellowship, South Africa

"It seems that over history the pendulum of Spirit and Word has swung harshly to the right or the left. Sadly, they are sometimes viewed as opposing thoughts in the Body of Christ. In *When Spirit and Word Collide*, Jarrod has married these two truths (for that is what they are) to reveal the value and importance of having them both to see God flourish in our communities.

This book is about a marriage – two different 'beings' who have the same heart and so come together to make a union work. The marriage of Spirit and Word, so vital, one as important as the other; one cannot truly thrive without the other.

As someone who has had the privilege of ministering in both highly traditional churches and the more prophetic, free form, 'messy', charismatic culture of Pentecostal expressions, I find this book refreshing in it's approach, valuing a healthy marriage of Word and Spirit as the emerging Church of this season.

I highly recommend this book from a person who isn't

just observing it, but living it."
Roma Waterman, Author of The God Artist and Releasing Heaven's Song, worship leader/songwriter/teacher

"Jarrod is part of a new generation who are 'standing on the shoulders' of those who have gone before, learning from them, but also willing to ask the hard questions, take risks and pay the cost. Jarod is speaking from several years of both travelling and local ministry and is now the senior pastor of a church in Hull. He is not the cowboy who rides through town and then leaves – he has worked through the stuff, warts and all, and can speak out of his own deep experience about what it means to lead a growing church.

What he has to say is, at times, uncomfortable, but it is right and he is someone who is honest enough to say that he is still learning. He says, 'As a pastor I do not exist to get people into church but into Christ' and this sums up everything. Read and be challenged, and prepare for some radical changes."
Norman Barnes, Founder of Links International

"*When Spirit and Word Collide* resounds with an inspiring and yet practical message that grips the heart. Delivered with a fresh perspective and insightful teaching, you will be challenged to re-evaluate what God can do through a generation that desire to see His glory."
Evangelist Nathan Morris, Shake The Nations Ministries

"Within the pages of this book, Jarrod's two great passions emerge: namely a commitment to the reality of God's Word and the power of His Spirit. As Word and Spirit are

authentically experienced within the Church, and through the Church expressed to a dying world, so God's glory will be revealed. This is a book birthed from a heart on fire and has the power to kindle a flame within all who read it."
Dr John Andrews, Principal of Mattersey Hall College and Graduate School

"My friend Jarrod Cooper is onto something very important in this book. When the authority of the Word collides with the power of the Spirit, there's an explosion of miraculous creativity which has the potential to influence nations towards God. Sit back and enjoy it. But don't get too comfortable. This is life changing stuff. You should read it."
Roy Todd, Speaker and author

"Jarrod is a friend who I admire greatly. He is the real deal! He has a deep and passionate desire for the UK and Europe to experience a genuine, fresh move of God. He has ordered his life and ministry believing this will happen. I began reading his book because I'd been asked to write a commendation, but I soon found myself highlighting sentences, musing and praying as I went from page to page. Jarrod writes from a place of humility and vulnerability with many years of ministry experience and yet a prophetic edge. His book is hope-filled, fresh and extremely practical. I believe it will be a handbook for many in ministry. We will use it here at All Nations as we seek to build and move forward in the coming season. I recommend it highly!"
Steve Uppal, Senior Leader, All Nations Church, Wolverhampton

Introduction

In 1947 a prophetic word was brought to the Body of Christ that most attribute to the man of faith, Smith Wigglesworth; a word that may change Church history. In it he spoke of several phases in the life of the Church that would span the decades following its utterance. Notably, for us today, the first few phases have unfolded exactly as prophesied. This makes the final, as yet unfulfilled, stage of his prophetic word of great interest to church leaders and all Christians today. Since the prophetic word has been so proven until now, we would be foolish to ignore its finale.

The series of teachings contained in this book have been birthed over the last decade, both from meditating on Wigglesworth's prophetic word and observing and studying revivals, outpourings and Church growth across the world.

In 1947 the great revivalist of faith prophesied the following:

"During the next few decades there will be two distinct moves of the Holy Spirit across the Church in Great Britain.

The first move will affect every church that is open to receive it, and will be characterised by a restoration of the baptism and gifts of the Holy Spirit.

The second move of the Holy Spirit will result in people leaving historic churches and planting new churches.

In the duration of each of these moves, the people who are involved will say, 'This is a great revival.' But the Lord says, 'No, neither is this the great revival but both are steps towards it.'

When the new church phase is on the wane, there will be evidence in the churches of something that has not been seen before: a coming together of those with an emphasis on the Word and those with an emphasis on the Spirit. When the Word and the Spirit come together, there will be the biggest move of the Holy Spirit that the nation, and indeed, the world has ever seen. It will mark the beginning of a revival that will eclipse anything that has been witnessed within these shores, even the Wesleyan and Welsh revivals of former years. The outpouring of God's Spirit will flow over from the United Kingdom to mainland Europe, and from there, will begin a missionary move to the ends of the earth."

If we were to look at this incredible prophetic word and apply it to seasons in the British Church (and, in many cases, the worldwide Church), those who know their recent Church history would verify the accuracy of this word up to now.

Without a doubt the first wave of God's Spirit has taken place and resulted in fresh outpourings in the older Pentecostal churches and renewal among Anglican and other historic denominations.

The second wave of planting new churches has also taken place, as was demonstrated by the House Church and Restoration movements bursting upon the scene.

In both cases these significant steps forward were heralded as revivals − confirming Smith's words that we would think of them as revivals, though they were not.

When the New Churches Wane

In the prophecy, Smith's mention of these two phases is followed by the words, "When the new church phase is on the wane..." This is something that has been underway for several years. The newest expressions of Church, along with historic denominations, have been facing similar struggles and a need for renewal. The pioneering edge that launched these movements is not quite what it used to be. (I realise that this statement is a broad brush stroke and there are always exceptions. In the main, however, many leaders testify to its truth).

This means that we are currently living in the "when" that Smith prophesied.

What happens when "the new churches wane"? Smith speaks of a coming move of God where Word people and Spirit people will come together, leading to, "the beginning of a revival that will eclipse anything that has been witnessed within these shores, even the Wesleyan and Welsh revivals of former years."

This statement is huge! Lest we gloss over its significance, the Welsh Revival brought over 100,000 people to Christ, transformed the nation and, along with Azusa Street, sparked modern Pentecostalism. Before this, the Wesleyan Revival ushered a fifth of the population to Christ and altered the core structure of our nation! So this is no small claim Smith makes. He believed a great awakening was due to hit our shores, the like of which no one has ever seen nor history book recorded.

This book is all about these people of the Spirit and the Word coming together to welcome God's Kingdom and build Spirit-filled churches in this amazing season, under the leadership of our Great Architect, God Himself. It is about a last days Church that will be glorious and powerful; simultaneously an organised army, a supernatural sign and a loving family.

Days of Wonder

In my first book, *Glory in the Church*, I wrote of my own encounter with God's glory, which burned a vision of a Church in revival across the UK into my soul:

"In 1996 I encountered the glory of God in a six-week visit to South Africa. During that time I was filled with a vision for the United Kingdom and Europe. Night after night I awoke, day after day I prayed, and visions of a great revival were burned into my heart. I am convinced the Church must be ready to host a glory at a level previously unknown.

The presence of God is preparing to sweep across Europe as never seen before. It will be in response to the apostolic reformation currently underway. Stadiums, arenas and the greatest auditoriums will be turned into church buildings. Marketplaces, filled with thousands, will be overcome by the glory of God. The blind will see. The lame will walk. Street evangelism will happen as never before, as mass healings take place on street corners and in shopping centres. Where many have spent years sowing, others will reap on a massive scale.

God's glory will touch the media, politics and royalty. His glory will invade live TV shows, as men and women of God reveal the power of God in healings, strange signs and prophetic words and wisdom. Many politicians will come to Christ in a very visible way. For some this will bring prominence, for others ridicule and scandal. Governments and kings will call days of prayer.

Thousands will stream into the Kingdom of God as a great move of signs and wonders floods our churches, workplaces and homes. Some believers will be transfigured as Moses was. Trances, dreams and visions will become commonplace. The weather will be controlled by believers at certain times, and used as a sign to communities where they are ministering. Neighbours will knock on the doors of those known to be Christians, begging to be led to Christ and to find peace for their souls. Many businesses and workplaces will hold prayer meetings; some will even close for whole days of prayer. Study groups will meet at all hours of the day in business establishments.

The glory of God will fill the greatest auditoriums in the land as Christians try to find places to gather that can contain the numbers flooding into the Kingdom. Great and glorious signs and wonders will be performed by apostolic teams, though even the least among the Church will see miracles as commonplace. Churches will be planted on a daily basis. Leaders will be trained quickly and released easily. Youngsters will lead churches of thousands. A softening of hearts between generations in churches will mean all ages will worship and walk together."

In this book I want to continue the story of my own

learning, failing, attempting and dreaming to see a Church birthed across Europe that will transform the social, political and spiritual landscape with God's glory.

I am, of course, full of questions and longings and these eclipse my answers and wisdom. Yet I share what I feel and know with you in the hope that together we can navigate this incredible season with all the grace and insight the Comforter provides.

I have a deep longing for so much more than I am living in right now. If you have a similar thirst to grow as a man or woman of God, as a leader, or in church or ministry, then read on ... we may just be the generation Smith was talking about. And if we are, it's about to get exciting!

Jarrod Cooper

1. Humble Pie
Never Tasted so Good

"A revival means days of heaven on earth."
Dr Martyn Lloyd-Jones

In the autumn of 2011 a magazine was published which blazed a headline quoting me. It said, "I believe in revival, but not that God will fall out the sky!" It contained an interview conducted months before where I had spoken of my belief that great days are ahead for the Church. But at the same time I had become sceptical of streams that constantly waited for a greater day, somewhere around the corner. I wanted to live that day *now*. I think I had concluded that it was better to call today "it", rather than expect more.

You see, Revival had seemed strangely out of reach in my 40 years of experience. Leaders I respected stated that if we only prayed a bit more, repented a bit more, lived a bit holier, then the tantalising revival cure-all would eventually come and sweep our nation. But "it" never really came.

Years passed by and as a leader I came to feel I would

much rather see a steady improvement, a gentle growing of the Church in strength and impact, until we were indeed a glorious bride for Christ.

As leader of a church, I had seen (and experienced!) that hope, constantly deferred, makes the heart sick (Proverbs 13:12). Unfulfilled dreams can be a hope destroyer. Better to live today well, I thought, than expect the "magic wand" of revival tomorrow!

Hence my lack of anticipation that God might simply "fall out of the sky" one day.

And it's here that God tripped me up.

I was wrong.

Perhaps not in every sense of my thinking, but I was wrong to think that God would not walk into a situation and do a "Solomon's Glory-filled Temple" job on us today; taking over the programme, overwhelming bodies, rushing through a community with salvation, healing, restoring, reviving!

Here's how it's started to happen...

God Will Come Like The Rain

"As surely as the sun rises, he will appear; he will come to us like the winter rains, like the spring rains that water the earth." (Hosea 6:3)

It's August 2011. I'm picking up some of our youth from a service and I find a few of them utterly overwhelmed by the Spirit of God, with no human intervention. It was nothing to do with the service they'd just been in. They were just laid out on the floor, barely able to rise, intoxicated with God. We've often seen people overwhelmed by the Spirit at times, but this was of another order.

To me, it was like a cloud the size of a man's hand. A small, unusual sign, that meant something was coming.

A few weeks later we were holding a last minute event, which I happened to name "God Will Come Like the Rain", based on scriptures in Psalms and Hosea where God promises to literally, "COME LIKE THE RAIN" ("fall out of the sky" you could say?).

And that is exactly what God did. Healings, salvations, backsliders on fire for God, and atmosphere, incredible atmosphere; like I had never known in 40 years of church life.

It was as if the smog of dull religion had been blown away in a divine rain storm! For several months God swept through our church transforming us and the ripples continued for many months and beyond.

God is still a Mover and Shaker!

As a leader who wants healthy, whole people, drawn into a grounded, loving, growing community, I had forgotten that while all that is indeed good, God is still a revolutionary mover and shaker. The lack of remarkable corporate visitation in my community had led me to reinvent my theology to fit our circumstances. I thought "God doesn't powerfully visit any more, He just gently inhabits."

I had dulled my thinking to fit my reality and concluded that God doesn't fall out of the sky, blow like a rushing wind, stir like a bubbling spring inside people any more. He doesn't hang in the air over a city or region for a period of time. He might visit a person, or give us a powerful weekend ... but can He literally pour out His Spirit on a region for months or years in new ways? I thought not.

Perhaps I had forgotten my Church history, because He

has done all that repeatedly in the last 2,000 years. In fact, almost every revolutionary development in Church life and growth has been accompanied by an overwhelming visitation of God's presence.

We often seem to fall into the trap of thinking of God as some Jedi-like force that we are able to tap into – rather than as a Person, someone who sees, interacts, dances, hugs, spins, shouts, whispers, roars, rains and shines. These are all scriptural pictures of God and they reveal His Ways. He moves in VARIOUS ways, at various times, in various places. Differently. Uniquely. Not equally. And God will continue to visit us in fresh, history-making ways, as He did in Wesley's day, the Welsh revival, Azusa Street, Argentina, China.

While in one sense God is always moving, and much of that movement is gentle and often hidden, He will also still burst on the scene in controversial power. He will do so in particular geographical locations, at certain times, usually annoying the "mainstream" and igniting the edges. He does love to annoy theologians in this way!

And so, I believe that in the years to come, again and again, rainstorms of God's power will continue to pour out in locations, for special seasons. Whether your theology or experience fits that or not, it's happening – globally. As sure as spring follows winter, moves of God will, and are, ebbing and flowing across the world.

Church leaders are naturally reticent to simply jump on board with the next "thing". Leaders know that while some outpourings are healthy, God-driven movements, others are hyped-up and in reality are unhealthy and shallow. But just because some outpourings are man-made imitations, that does not alter the fact that God can outpour Himself like rain.

So how do we prepare for such moves as men and women of God? As church leaders? How can we experience healthy Spirit-filled movements? Does "revival" have to mean nightly meetings or is there a healthier "model" to adopt when God begins to move in such a way? How can we live in the healthy, true movement of God and avoid all the shallow hype?

2. When Spirit and Word Unite

"There are two ways of being united – one is by being frozen together and the other is by being melted together. What Christians need is to be united in brotherly love, and then they may expect to have power."

D.L. Moody

Wigglesworth prophesied there would be "a coming together of those with an emphasis on the Word and those with an emphasis on the Spirit." I am quite sure that most within Word and Spirit spheres consider themselves to have achieved the right balance between Word and Spirit (it's amazing how easily we set ourselves up as the benchmark for balance, myself included!) But what did Smith (or more importantly, God) mean by this statement? And what might the fulfilment of this prophecy look like? At the risk of appearing too subjective in my views, can I first offer some possible definitions of those who are Word orientated and Spirit orientated.

I think this will help clarify where each of us sits on the

spectrum. Can you see yourself/your church?

The Spirit Streams

I would say that Spirit orientated streams/churches/leaders are generally:

- Seeing or pursuing a regular flow of healings, prophecy and miracles, both in private and public settings
- Expect a more open and spontaneous flow of the Spirit in their meetings. They find it difficult to predict an "end time" to their services (and for this reason struggle with multiple services)
- Their worships bands don't follow a specific set list/ song list, but expect a more free flowing, improvised, "following the Spirit" approach. Speaking and/or singing in tongues will be a feature of public worship times.
- Often the Spirit church longs for the time when they will have to put on nightly meetings, such is the intensity of God's presence.

The Word Streams

I would say that Word orientated streams/churches/ leaders tend to be:

- Strong on and excellent at preaching the Word
- Have great discipleship programmes, good growth, and can handle multiple services
- Have more of a focus on social action
- Are well organised, often contemporary, and place a high value on excellence in all they do. Meetings start and end on time most of the time!
- Have a far more structured approach to worship (and

meetings in general, with things tied down well ahead of time). Worship songs are selected and prepared in advance, thus releasing the ability to coordinate lighting, computer technology and audio visual effects.

- Possibly the last thing the Word church wants is nightly meetings. Their goal is to see a great church community built and worry about "camping out" around some phenomenon, which is potentially exciting, but at the same time exhausting for staff and members alike

These are, of course, very broad brush strokes and even as I write, there are both Word and Spirit churches who are blending the best of both ends of the spectrum in order to embrace the benefits of one another's culture. This "coming together" is what this book is all about.

Why do Word and Spirit churches need each other?

Each of the qualities listed above are the "upsides" of the Word and Spirit emphases. In a sense they are both "correct" in their approach. Both approaches bring blessing. But both approaches may also limit the fullness of God's purposes for His Church.

The Downsides

Both emphases are needed in order to achieve the dynamic churches God desires. While each emphasis has strength in it, a counterbalance is needed in order for such a church to fully express the glory God intends.

For instance, many Spirit-orientated churches tend to be poorly organised and therefore small. There can be a fear (even a demonization!) of organisation, lest the freedom of the Holy Spirit is quenched. Ultimately, this can lead to poor pastoring, care and outreach, since doing this for large numbers requires a good measure of organisation.

Then, without the grounding of a strong biblical teaching gift, which "pulls" believers towards a balanced centre, people can focus on the fringes. The prophetic guys can embrace stuff that is whacky and flaky.

And endless hankering after a revival that is somewhere around the corner can leave people burned out and disillusioned when it never seems to happen – or at least not on the scale people would like. Consequently, in Spirit churches, much time can be consumed praying for revival without actually doing anything about it. They may spend less time reaching the lost and more time focusing on prayer as the key to church growth. But this growth rarely occurs with any significance, with most churches hitting the glass ceiling of around 120 members, and often much lower.

Being better organised, Word churches tend to become larger and therefore more influential. But often, whilst the numbers of people can make them feel exciting, these churches are often lacking in spiritual power. They are not as presence filled and may inhibit the moving of the Holy Spirit, since their methods of ministry are more rigid and prescriptive.

The Bible describes God's Spirit as being like the wind, like oil, like a fire, like water – He moves where He will, is unpredictable and cannot be contained. Thus, in Word orientated churches where predictability and tight organisation are championed, miracles are much less frequent (or non-existent).

Whilst a degree of organisation is good and necessary, too much and services become more reliant upon the skilled use of multimedia to create an atmosphere. Worship can become formulaic – a "three fast songs, followed by three slow songs" pattern that doesn't allow for any spontaneity.

Dare I say that, in some churches, God is almost "not allowed" to turn up in His glory and do what He wants – so He doesn't! Word-orientated church leaders, who openly say things like, "I don't really understand the miraculous" abound, in my experience. Some even make fun of the miraculous. They have confided in me that they often have very little prayer culture, little or no expectation of miracles happening, and that the flow of prophecy is restricted to leadership and planning settings. There is sadly little value placed on the gifts of the Spirit that the apostle Paul told us to "earnestly desire, crave and pursue" (1 Corinthians 14:1).

The Extremes Are Being Drawn Together
In times past, exponents of both the Word and Spirit emphases have defended the rightness of their respective positions with a harsh arrogance. But times are changing. I sense we are finally putting our spiritual L-plates back on and realising that it's time to come together and see large, well organised, miracle working, Word and Spirit-filled churches populating our land.

In this season the following quote is ringing in my ears:

"In times of change learners inherit the earth, while the learned find themselves beautifully prepared for a world that no longer exists." – Eric Hoffer

A shift is taking place. It's time to admit that none of us has all the answers, soften our hearts, and listen to the wisdom, experience and expertise of brothers who inhabit cultures different to our own. We all have something to learn.

It's Happening

Many senior national leaders are saying they are experiencing a coming together of Spirit and Word people as never before, in their regional and national forums. There is an increasing hunger to learn how to build church with both values in full flow.

So, what might a true Spirit and Word church look like? How can the two emphases be drawn together to achieve the ideal balance? This is what I've observed...

1. Word and Spirit churches are responsive and adaptable

There is an ebb and flow of dynamics. One week you may think you're in a contemporary "attractional" service, and the next there is a flow of the Spirit with spontaneous manifestations of God's power! One week your church feels like Hillsong, the next like Bethel, Redding. One month you're digesting brilliant theology, the next you're overwhelmed by glory!

2. Word and Spirit churches are flexible

You are brilliantly organised, but tender and supple to "late notice" from the Holy Spirit. Spontaneity and planning walk in honour of each other. There is a joy in the church's ability to flow between the two dynamics. The Holy Spirit always remains Lord, but planning is designed to give room for spontaneity.

3. Word and Spirit churches are sensitive

As the Holy Spirit moves, occasionally strange things might happen as the prophetic breaks out. But these things are explained in common language, and with love for those who may potentially be confused. Though we're never aiming to be offensive or unusual, God's Might and Mystery are not hidden behind a contemporary mask of "cool". (Though we are cool! Remember, you get no brownie points for living in the 80s. PLEASE take down your felt banners!)

4. Word and Spirit churches are organised but not restricted

Excellence in creative art, contemporary sound, stagecraft and design exists in partnership with healing, miracles, glory and reaching out to the lost.

5. Word and Spirit churches are presence-centred, but not presence-obsessed

A sense of God's presence is a characteristic of Word and Spirit meetings, but not every meeting has to be spectacular. You can make regular visits to a mountaintop, but you can't live there permanently. In fact, it's unhealthy to think you can live there.

6. Word and Spirit churches promote balanced living

There is equal emphasis placed upon spiritual power and spiritual discipline. Leaders model and exemplify the miraculous, Spirit-filled life, publicly and privately, but recognise that lives are built on the Word of God and through consistent discipleship, not one-off phenomena. Therefore, there is a coming together of regular discipleship programmes, combined with an openness towards and engagement with the Holy Spirit.

If We Come Together...

If Word and Spirit churches can come together across the

nation, stream joining with stream to become a river, Word leader arm in arm with Spirit leader, to build the Church with both an apostolic and prophetic emphasis then, as Wigglesworth prophesied, the result will be:

"The biggest move of the Holy Spirit that the nation, and indeed, the world has ever seen. It will mark the beginning of a revival that will eclipse anything that has been witnessed within these shores, even the Wesleyan and Welsh revivals of former years. The outpouring of God's Spirit will flow over from the United Kingdom to mainland Europe and, from there, will begin a missionary move to the ends of the earth."

Coming together doesn't mean we must all look the same, or must embrace the entire fullness of each other's emphasis. But there is a warming to each other; a coming together; a realisation that we need each other.

We don't all have to sing the same melody and be identical in all areas of style – our differences are wonderful and powerful in and of themselves – but we should all sing in harmony: one unique, God-given emphasis comprising all our unique callings working together.

The Bones and the Breath

"The hand of the LORD was on me, and he brought me out by the Spirit of the Lord and set me in the middle of a valley; it was full of bones. He led me back and forth among them, and I saw a great many bones on the floor of the valley, bones that were very dry. He asked me, 'Son of man, can these bones live?'

I said, 'Sovereign Lord, you alone know.'

Then he said to me, 'Prophesy to these bones and say

to them, "Dry bones, hear the word of the Lord! This is what the Sovereign Lord says to these bones: I will make breath enter you, and you will come to life. I will attach tendons to you and make flesh come upon you and cover you with skin; I will put breath in you, and you will come to life. Then you will know that I am the Lord."'

So I prophesied as I was commanded. And as I was prophesying, there was a noise, a rattling sound, and the bones came together, bone to bone. I looked, and tendons and flesh appeared on them and skin covered them, but there was no breath in them.

Then he said to me, 'Prophesy to the breath; prophesy, son of man, and say to it, "This is what the Sovereign Lord says: Come, breath, from the four winds and breathe into these slain, that they may live."' So I prophesied as he commanded me, and breath entered them; they came to life and stood up on their feet—a vast army." (Ezekiel 37:1-10)

Here the prophet Ezekiel is told to prophesy to bones and flesh and then to the breath. Together the combination of bones, flesh and breath creates a powerful, strong army, able to do all that God desires. Without breath, the army exists, but is not alive. Without bones, the army is alive, but unable to move and fight!

It is the same with the Church. Every church needs to have bones and breath; wineskin as well as wine; Word as well as Spirit. We need both organisation and spontaneity; skill and intimacy; wisdom and wonder.

In the tension of these different truths, types, styles or gifts, we will find, I believe, godly maturity and will experience the full power of heaven.

So, for the remainder of this book I want to talk about areas of bones (organisation and skill) and breath (spirituality and gift) that need to be awakened in every church that seeks to be fully Christlike. Each of them are "revivals" that need to take place within our churches.

A revival of our bones (or the wineskin) will include organisation, skills, wisdom, structure, authority, planning and methods. Jesus said He would "build" His Church — that is a feat of engineering, a skilled work.

A revival of our breath (or the outpoured wine of heaven) speaks of renewed intimacy, presence, atmosphere, prophetic movement and power. The early Church experienced an outpouring of the rushing wind of heaven — that is a work of intimacy, a Spirit work.

I'm sure some of us will immediately resonate with certain chapters that follow, knowing that they are already our strengths and preferences. Perhaps then we should take more note of the chapters we might like to dismiss? Those may be the very places in which we need reviving.

Some will love the talk of organisation and leadership. I would suggest then, reading more slowly and prayerfully the chapters on intimacy, presence and power.
Others will immediately love the talk of presence, power and prophecy. Similarly, perhaps it would be wise to read more slowly the chapters on organisation and growth, before dismissing them as contrary to a true Spirit-filled church. I pray the pages of this book might inspire some missing segment in your spirit and mine, to awaken us more fully to any areas we are inclined to overlook. As I have studied, taught and written on these areas in recent years, I have been surprised at how much defensive, poor

theology I have used to cover my laziness or preferences. I have also been disappointed at the "lens of envy" I have used to judge streams that did not do things as I would, making me harsh and dismissive of some great truths that are modelled in those streams.

But as I have travelled, read, prayed and pondered, God has chipped away at my hardness of heart and brought me to new perspectives I never imagined I'd hold. Perhaps you too could be on the same journey? You and I may be right where Smith prophesied: on the brink of a coming together as never before; on the brink of a Great Revival.

3. A Revival
of Pentecost

*"The path of the righteous is like the first gleam of dawn,
shining ever brighter till the full light of day."*
(Proverbs 4:18)

Jesus' parting commission to 11 of His disciples to blaze
the Good News of Salvation through every nation came
complete with authenticating signs of that Gospel. He
didn't just give them a mission, He described the culture
that would accompany it. In Mark 16:17 He states:

*"Those who believe will drive out demons, speak in
tongues, heal the sick and know supernatural protection."*

Jesus fully expected His Church to display these
remarkable signs of validation – the hallmarks of heaven
– which would attract attention to the message, as well as
expressing His love and compassion for the hurting.

When John the Baptist sought to identify Jesus as
the Christ, he enquired from prison, *"Are you the One?"*
(Matthew 11:3). Jesus reply was simply, *"Tell him what you
see: the blind see, the lame walk, the deaf hear, the dead*

are raised." His divine call was evidenced by more than words. Heaven was coming to earth where He walked.

Similarly, Paul stated that, *"The Kingdom of God is not a matter of talk, but power"* (1 Corinthians 4:20).

This is, of course, a huge challenge to many of us leaders and churches today. It questions us to the core and calls us to examine our personal walk, the depth of our spirituality, our call, our faith, our authenticity.

Some shy away from the issue of supernatural signs, but even the most cursory reading of the book of Acts makes it quite clear that miraculous phenomena are a true, acceptable, essential part of church life. They are not something to be ashamed of or dismissed as belonging to the "flaky" fringes of church life.

According to Jesus, signs and wonders should be embraced by the majority – part and parcel of our reaching the world. The miraculous is not for the minority – it must be mainstream. He fully expected us to enjoy *"signs following"* (Mark 16:17).

Not Just a Commission, But a Culture

So how, with all our great preaching, wonderful music, necessary social action and "attractional" models of Church, can we ensure that we are fulfilling Jesus' divine commission to the full? Not just preaching the gospel to the lost, but establishing a divine culture through supernatural means. How can the gifts of the Spirit operate with integrity in a contemporary church setting? Can our Apostles leave us filled with the wonder of heaven once again?

Endless fabulous books exist about good use of the gifts of the Spirit, so I don't want to repeat the absolute basics, but here are some thoughts I believe we'll need to embrace to experience God's glory in our churches once again:

1. The Power of Offence

Firstly, to all those who are nervous of the "image" of the supernatural aspect of ministry, we must remember there is an offence to the gospel we simply can't avoid. Whether it's the strangeness of the gifts of the Spirit, or the abrasiveness of the call to repentance, the gospel is not easy. It's not politically correct, man-made, and certainly not politely British! But we must also remember that history proves our world respects truthful challenge more than political correctness.

If we look back at the effects of early Methodism – through which some report that up to a fifth of our nation was saved, lifted out of poverty and brought into meaningful Christian communities – we see that this was achieved in an atmosphere of radical preaching and a powerful sense of God's presence. Old Methodist pulpits had "escape doors", since the congregation would often rush forward violently to attack preachers who were ablaze with truth! As John Wesley calmly preached, people writhed, cried out and fell to the ground. Yet despite persecution and countercultural zeal, Wesley died a hero of the nation, loved and appreciated by millions in his day. Great, challenging moves of God will do more for our nation than tidy Christianity.

As G K Chesterton said: "We don't want a Church that moves with the world, we want a Church that moves the world." A strong, confident, supernatural Church has always been the fulfilment of this, not a fashionable Church.

2. The Power of Presence

Let's also remind ourselves that Church history shows that each historic revival and reformation carried with it an incredible atmosphere, not simply a truth. God's powerful presence was manifest. When Wesley preached in the fields, young men would fall out of the trees, overwhelmed by God. Trembling, falling to the ground and open confessions of sin were common. On the day of Pentecost, such an atmosphere swept 3,000 people into the kingdom, at the challenging words of Peter. The simple proximity of Charles Finney brought factory workers to their knees when he passed by. "Atmosphere" is not just the passion that comes from having a vision, or the natural excitement of putting on a good event – it is pure heaven unleashed through men and women of God who are on fire!

3. The Power of Hunger

Without doubt, in order to see such moves of God in our nation again, someone, somewhere has to passionately desire it. John 7:37-38 makes it clear that for the Spirit to be present, there must be a thirst, a hunger, for such a move of God. Paul urged us to, *"eagerly desire spiritual gifts"*. Often we are too passive, saying to God, "Well, if it's your will, Lord, let me have your spiritual gifts." In fact, God wants us to desire them. The first requirement for receiving the gifts is a hunger for them. Are we truly, biblically, HUNGRY for them, in our personal spiritual lives, in our church congregations? A challenging thought.

4. A Listening Ear

Next, the presence of God is not simply a feeling. I LOVE

to feel Him, but the true power of the presence is found in discovering God's voice. One gentle whisper from God and I know what to do. Jesus did, *"whatever he saw his father doing"* (John 5:19). Jesus chose not to enact His own ideas, opting for complete dependence upon and obedience to His father, doing *"nothing of himself"*. In our "copy and paste" formulaic ministry world, this presents a further challenge. Are we dwelling in God's presence, seeking His direction and listening to His voice, or acting from our own initiative? Are we ministering out of intimacy or imitation?

5. An Obedient Heart

The power of God is always found in the instruction of God. Whether it is, *"March around the walls"* (Joshua 6:3), *"Go wash in the Jordan"* (2 Kings 5:10) or *"Lift your staff over the sea"* (Exodus 14:16), God's power is released as we obey His voice. This means that our meetings and ministries must become more geared towards hearing God's voice than fulfilling a programme we have designed. We need to be more concerned about the whisper of heaven than the tick of a clock.

6. A Passionate Faith

A guest speaker came to our church and, in the very first meeting, with no hype and no "build up" in order to get people's faith going, pulled a woman out of her wheelchair, who was miraculously healed. Around 250 leaders were gathered for a leader's forum. Many arrived with a, "Been there, done that, got the t-shirt" look on their faces, but after this, suddenly everyone was on their feet, yelling and dancing around – transformed, all because one man brought passionate faith back to the party!

The woman returned to the hotel where she had booked in as an invalid, hours before, and promptly led the Muslim receptionist to the Lord! We will never see the miraculous without a return to passionate, bold faith. Read Joshua 1 and you will see that four times Joshua was told to *"be bold, be strong"*. The same applies to us if we want to enter God's fullness. A Church without boldness is a Church without miracles!

7. A Fearless Heart

The fear of man is probably the greatest hindrance to the gifts of healing, knowledge, signs and wonders. At a recent service I felt God say that there was a man present who had two hearing aids in, who God wanted to heal. Hearing God like this and then stepping out in faith to act upon that word always carries with it an element of risk. We need to have an utter disregard for our own reputation if we are going to move in the gifts. In this situation, it was no good me being paralysed by the fear of, "What if this doesn't work?" I gave out the word of knowledge and a man responded. After 25 years of profound deafness, he can now hear whispers!

Since then, in the last 9 months over 28 people have been healed of deafness at our church, and everyone took a leap of faith! Someone, somewhere has to start living a life that cares less for our reputation and more for His kingdom to come!

8. A Genuine Love for People

Of course, miracles are never about the glitz of platform ministry. In reality, they are about love. Love for people.

God's love to lift people out of sickness and despair. They are God's "Love Signs" to accompany the challenge and grace of the gospel. Without love in our pursuit of the gifts we are just noisy cymbals, banging gongs (1 Corinthians 13).

9. Heaven's Expression of Love

Love cannot stop at social action, vital though that is. Jesus' most common social action activity was to heal people through miracles. Could we express social action the same way? Can we develop that same compassionate boldness that tackles cancer, chronic injury and debilitating sickness, and gives people their lives and dignity back? What could be more loving?

A young man came to our church in a wheelchair. He was also deaf, due to a stroke and a bad fall. One Thursday evening he was pulled out of his wheelchair, healed of his deafness, and completely restored! He had to hand back his disability car, start a business, and that very night was able to "carry his wife over the threshold" for the first time, as they entered their home! Miracles are not just a phenomenon, they are heaven's compassion at work; God giving dignity and wholeness to restore families, marriages and individual's destinies.

10. A Return to the Source

So where do we go to find all this power? Where have the gifts gone? Where is His voice? Where are the wonders? I believe that if we are to return to the biblical culture of signs and wonders, we must return to the biblical source of them – the outpouring of the Holy Spirit on, in and through the Church! If we get the source right, the gifts will naturally flow.

On the Day of Pentecost the believers looked as though they were drunk (Acts 2:13), overwhelmed by God's presence. Two chapters later they were seeking Him and being filled once again. The result? Boldness, signs, wonders, awe, fear and multiplication!

Whether we speak of revivals of Wales and Azusa street, of Wesley and John G Lake, of the revivals of China, South America or parts of Africa, we find that they were all deeply acquainted with the Source – God's powerful presence! Every great revival has been accompanied by a powerful outpouring of heaven. Every church, every leader, every Christian, needs their own, regular "Pentecost".

Our greatest danger is that we simply fill the various "slots" of our meeting without connecting with heaven. We allocate some time to worship, playing through our song list, then we preach our tidy sermons. This soon descends into religion, when what we need is another Pentecost; another infusion of Heaven. When the Holy Spirit comes upon a church, or a preacher, a young mum, or a youth group, the gifts will naturally flow. Wisdom will flow in prophecy and knowledge. Hands will be placed on sick bodies and sickness will leave. Demons will cry out and depart. Miraculous tongues will be uttered. And we shall look like the Church Jesus commissioned and described in Mark 16.

Worship in Vain

Jesus spoke about the danger of long-term "religious" leadership when He addressed a group of Pharisees, the religious leaders of the day, in Mark 7:

"Isaiah was right when he prophesied about you hypocrites; as it is written: 'These people honour me with their lips, but their hearts are far from me. They worship me in vain; their teachings are merely human rules.' You have let go of the commands of God and are holding on to human traditions."

First Jesus called them hypocrites, literally "actors". "You're play-acting," He tells them. "Going through the religious motions."

He then describes how that happens:

"You let go of God's commands and get stuck in tradition." Eugene Peterson puts it this way in The Message paraphrase: "They just use me as a cover for teaching whatever suits their fancy."

Leaders can be in danger of building a church that "suits their fancy". We design it around our preferences, around our gift, our comfort zone. For some, the question "What is going to bring growth?" is a bigger priority than "What is healthy?" or "Is God's kingdom coming in our midst?" We are not after growth at any cost. We are after healthy, heavenly growth. We must not simply get people into church, but into Christ!

Sadly, Jesus says that the humanising of our thinking makes our worship "in vain". A great waste of time. If we are not building churches that are infused with the Spirit, as Jesus and the early apostles taught, then we are in danger of designing a work of vanity. Please God, keep us from wasting our time.

So how, as leaders, can we start our journey back to (or deeper into) the source of God's power and, in turn, build the kind of Church He desires in the 21st Century?

4. A Revival of Intimacy

"Men may spurn our appeals, reject our message, oppose our arguments, despise our persons – but they are helpless against our prayers."
Sidlow Baxter

I play golf. Badly.

After hacking around a golf course for a few years I decided to get myself and my dad some lessons. On our first lesson the instructor asked me to show him my "swing". I took my untrained position over the ball, had a swing, and was actually quite chuffed that I hit the ball and hit it straight!

"Okay," the instructor encouraged, as he moved in on me. Manhandling my body, he started grabbing me and moving me about.

"Now, let's just move your feet to there, your back to here, your hands more like this, and your head here. Now swing."

I swung again. The ball went twice as far!

Tiny changes in my posture utterly transformed my game.

Small changes, big results!

It's the same with ministry. We are often deceived into thinking it's going to take massive, life-altering changes in order to see great developments in our churches, an increase of power in our ministries, an increase in miracles, the growth of our disciples, or numerical growth in our church. Yet Jesus teaches about small seeds moving great mountains; that children can own the kingdom; that the meek inherit the earth.

In the Kingdom of heaven, small hinges move great things. Little keys open great doors.

What is Your Posture?
Personally, the greatest "small change" in my world has been with regard to the "posture" I lead from. While we are almost pressured into developing successful churches by working from a place of leadership gifts, organisation or busyness (which can all be good in right measure), the Bible is really clear that senior leaders need to lead from a posture of prayer.

A Senior Leader's Job Description
"In those days when the number of disciples was increasing, the Hellenistic Jews among them complained against the Hebraic Jews because their widows were being overlooked in the daily distribution of food. So the Twelve gathered all the disciples together and said, 'It would not be right for us to neglect the ministry of the word of God in order to wait on tables. Brothers and sisters, choose seven

men from among you who are known to be full of the Spirit and wisdom. We will turn this responsibility over to them and will give our attention to prayer and the ministry of the word.' This proposal pleased the whole group ... So the word of God spread. The number of disciples in Jerusalem increased rapidly." (Acts 6:1-7).

In Acts 6 the apostles had a complaint brought to them: the church was growing, leading to increased need, but some people were getting left out of the daily distribution of food.

Today, many pastors would jump in to fix this problem, giving up an extra afternoon to do the work that needs doing. After all, it's an opportunity to model servant leadership, right? But here we find a different response.

The apostles are determined to defend their posture of prayerfulness and purposeful preaching:

"It would not be right for us to neglect the ministry of the word of God in order to wait on tables ... we will give our attention to prayer and the ministry of the word." (Acts 6:2-4)

The result of this brave stand to protect their true purpose was rapid church growth (Acts 6:7).

Intimacy with God in prayer, bringing the needs of my community to Him in intercession, listening to His voice for wisdom, preaching the Word from heaven – this is my primary call as a senior leader and I must defend that. When I do, tremendous power is available to me as a leader. And if the community I lead is to know God's power then no one is going to be as effective in modelling that than me. If my church is to have the countenance of Christ and the glory of God moving among her, then I need to make changes in my posture to lead primarily from a place of intimacy with God.

D L Moody was to have a campaign in England. An elderly pastor protested: "Why do we need this 'Mr Moody'? He's uneducated and inexperienced. Who does he think he is anyway? Does he think he has a monopoly on the Holy Spirit?"

A younger, wiser, pastor rose and responded, "No sir, but the Holy Spirit has a monopoly on Mr Moody."

Martin Luther said, "If I should neglect prayer but a single day, I should lose a great deal of the fire of faith."

As pastors today, do we let the Holy Spirit have a monopoly on our time? If we did, what effect would it have on our ministries? Can you truly say that you lead from a posture of prayer? Do you allow the whispers of heaven to bathe your soul in God's wisdom and plans? Are you off-loading all the pressures and difficulties to Him in prayer? This can be hardest thing to do when we are working almost alone, building up a work for God, trying to move a body of believers into a healthy place, and reach a community all at the same time.

Actually, the job isn't just hard – it's IMPOSSIBLE!

But the power we need is available. It doesn't come from copying and pasting what other successful leaders or churches have done (though God may give you revelation from some of those). It comes through getting God's grace and hearing God's mind on what you are to do, how you are to do it, and with whom.

Is prayer at the top of your job description? If it's not, you need to re-do your job spec and reorder your priorities.

I was writing a job description for a very senior position

in our church the other day, and knew I had turned a good corner when the top thing I placed on the duties was prayer. I was writing with the culture of heaven in mind (this has taken quite a journey!)

I didn't want or need a list of jobs doing, I wanted someone to bring a specific spiritual dimension to our ministry. I wasn't primarily seeking someone with great ideas, hard work or skills (though I need ALL of those!) but someone who is a man or woman of God, walking in the power of His Holy Spirit!

I believe we are entering a new day, where we are going to find success coming from a revival of intimacy with God among our leaders. The amount of senior leaders and apostles giving themselves to pray, to seek, to preach, to stay in God's presence and become conduits of His glory on earth, is going to increase. This is going to mean rapid growth, signs and wonders and impactful authority.

Some leaders are already saying that they are unavailable (except for emergencies) before 12 noon, and spending the first half of their work day in prayer. Others devote 2-3 specific days a week to prayer and study. Some church team members are being told that 20% of their work time is to be spent in prayer. Many have regular sabbaticals or days away to seek God and retreats away from the local work and scene.

Stand on the Ramparts

Habakkuk 2:1-2 speaks about a leader getting into the right posture for leading God's community:

"I will stand at my watch and station myself on the ramparts; I will look to see what he will say to me … Then

the Lord replied: 'Write down the revelation and make it plain on tablets so that a herald may run with it."

In years gone by, much church leadership has suffered from the "one man band" approach, but it is not a leader's job to run every project, meet every person, make every decision or do all the work. A leader's job is to be stationed in God's high presence, the place where he or she can see what God wants to do; a place where we can hear God's warnings, dreams, plans and pace.

Then the leader must make it clear, write it down (even decipher it sometimes!) and enable others to run with it. To do this we must become used to living "stationed on the ramparts", constantly on the lookout for God's direction; attentive to His voice; poised in the place of His presence; postured in the private place of prayer. From here all ministry of true eternal value flows.

If you desire to play a part in the coming move of God in our world, it will never be done without worship and intimacy. Valuing closeness and space with God, when we could be busy "doing a bit more", is paramount. A generation of leaders is going to find they will actually do a little less, but become many times more effective because of the power of God downloaded into their lives.

5. A Revival of Apostleship

"A New Testament apostolic function fully deployed within the Church today would significantly impact the dominion of darkness."
David Cannistraci

Where have all the miracle working apostles gone?

"They devoted themselves to the apostles' teaching and to fellowship, to the breaking of bread and to prayer. Everyone was filled with awe at the many wonders and signs performed by the apostles." (Acts 2:42-43)

These days it seems that the definition of the title "apostle" is someone who leads a big church, speaks on high profile platforms, or who leads fresh moves of church planting. Whilst I have nothing against any of those things, of course, these are not the biblical qualifications of an apostle. The Bible states that the things that mark an apostle are, "Signs, wonders and miracles, done among you with great perseverance." (2 Corinthians 12:12)

This is kind of un-missable. It's black and white. Apart

from the Cessationist theological viewpoint, I can't see how anyone could apply enough liberal thinking to get out of it.

Yet many (not all) of the UK's "apostles" I meet these days shy away from even attempting to see undeniable miracles in a public setting (Acts 2:43).

They usually argue that the provision for their building project was their "sign", the result of the preaching their "wonder", and the flow of wisdom in their leadership meetings the only required evidence of prophecy and the Spirit's moving. But I think that falls short of the scriptural example.

Miracle Workers

Acts 5 tells us a story that reveals a culture led by biblical apostles:

"The apostles performed many signs and wonders among the people. And all the believers used to meet together in Solomon's Colonnade. No one else dared join them, even though they were highly regarded by the people. Nevertheless, more and more men and women believed in the Lord and were added to their number. As a result, people brought the sick into the streets and laid them on beds and mats so that at least Peter's shadow might fall on some of them as he passed by. Crowds gathered also from the towns around Jerusalem, bringing their sick and those tormented by impure spirits, and all of them were healed."

One cannot argue with the fact that Jesus and the apostles of old had that supernatural ability to wade into a crowd of sick people and come out the other end with the lame walking, the blind seeing and some amazed faces! Where has that calibre of apostle gone? (Boy this challenges me!)

The impact of this "miracle shunning" apostleship in the Church will be far reaching if this nervousness of the supernatural isn't ended.

Firstly, there are those who will remain sick, or worse, die, because we have not been "as Christ in this world", doing "greater things than Jesus did" (John 14:12) and healed the sick among us. Only those who don't need a miracle would think of healing as unimportant! Ask a dying man for his perspective on miracles. He'll be hungry for more of God!

Secondly, since the Church is built on the foundation of apostles and prophets (Ephesians 2:20), the Church will inevitably reflect its leaders' strengths and weaknesses. I believe the lack of example of supernatural leadership will result in churches and congregations that are Cessationist in practice, though not in creed. We are currently in danger of raising a generation of young leaders in churches that think of themselves as "Spirit-filled", who have never tasted a move of God, seen a miracle or truly grasped or known the power of prophecy! Ultimately we will end up with a Church devoid of power.

Of course, God won't let this happen. I am personally encouraged by recent murmurings in movements which have shied away from the supernatural in recent decades, returning to a hunger for God's miraculous power among us. Words like "revival" and phrases like "moves of the Spirit" are becoming acceptable again in certain streams that ridiculed them in recent decades. This is a sign of Smith's prophesy coming true.

The Rise of New Apostles

In the coming decades we will see the emergence of apostles who carry a specific message from Christ, pioneer extraordinary church planting and missionary movements once again, and perform remarkable miracles in the public arena.

This in turn will release waves of fresh expectation and glory through the Church. We won't only pioneer great new worship or outreach methods, there will also be great upgrades of power and faith. Signs, wonders and miracles will flood even the Western Church. Truly, the greatest days of the Church are ahead of us not behind. God is going to write revival on the landscape of the United Kingdom, Europe and the world, as He releases these last days apostles to turn the word upside down, like the apostles of old!

Alongside a revival of intimacy with God and of miracle working apostleship, another surge of cultural transformation is taking place around the world...

6. A Revival
of Discipleship

"Those who aren't following Jesus aren't his followers. It's that simple. Followers follow, and those who don't follow aren't followers."
Scot McKnight

The next area God will revive in these coming decades is not so much about power, presence or intimacy, but rather about the character of our church members and the depth of our engagement in God's purposes. Ultimately, I believe He is going to transform what it means to be a church member.

God did not ask us to make "church members", count "decisions", or even have people say, "the sinner's prayer" (not that I'm against any of those things necessarily). He actually told us to be and to make *disciples*.

A church member in some of today's circles is more like the member of any social club. Some want to go to a certain church because it's cool, big, glitzy ... or because it's small, comfortable, not too demanding.

All this has little to do with the real walk of faith and the real JESUS.

Just read the following verses that show how Jesus thought of the journey of walking with Him:

"Jesus went up on a mountainside and called to him those he wanted, and they came to him. He appointed twelve that they might be with him and that he might send them out to preach." (Mark 3:13-14)

"As they were walking along the road, a man said to him, 'I will follow you wherever you go.' Jesus replied, 'Foxes have dens and birds have nests, but the Son of Man has no place to lay his head.' He said to another man, 'Follow me.' But he replied, 'Lord, first let me go and bury my father.' Jesus said to him, 'Let the dead bury their own dead, but you go and proclaim the kingdom of God.' Still another said, 'I will follow you, Lord; but first let me go back and say goodbye to my family.' Jesus replied, 'No one who puts a hand to the plow and looks back is fit for service in the kingdom of God.'" (Luke 9:57-62)

"Peter said to him, 'We have left all we had to follow you!' 'Truly I tell you,' Jesus said to them, 'no one who has left home or wife or brothers or sisters or parents or children for the sake of the kingdom of God will fail to receive many times as much in this age, and in the age to come eternal life.'" (Luke 18:28-29)

"Then Jesus said to his disciples, 'Whoever wants to be my disciple must deny themselves and take up their cross and

follow me. For whoever wants to save their life will lose it, but whoever loses their life for me will find it.'" (Matthew 16:24-25)

In the gospels we find that Jesus-followers entered into a deeply life changing arrangement. The disciples had to be...

...Available

Busy people gave up their jobs and plans to follow Jesus after a single request. Would you or I? He may not require everyone to give up their careers, but all will have to make space for the learning and mission of being a disciple.

...Teachable

Jesus told them, *"I will make you fishers of men."* It was clear He was going to teach them. A disciple, by inference, has a teacher. If you are the leader, that's you! Are we discipling our church members or filling in databases and doing hospital visits? Every church should be a training ground and every Christian a soldier either in, or preparing for, battle.

...Breakable

Talented Peter went through some deep, humbling experiences. Disciples accept humility and brokenness as part of the journey. Pride is at the root of all sin and must be winkled out. God will line all of us up for some rejection, failure and being overlooked. Are we teaching our people to handle it? Are we preaching brokenness and teaching repentance? Are we confronting sin? We've all got to pass that test (or keep retaking it!)

...Grace-able

A new word! By Acts 2 the disciples were humbled, prayerful and open to God's empowering presence. Grace was able to reach and empower them. They'd learned how to harness the wind of His presence. Are we modelling a prayerful Spirit-filled life of power to our people? Are we teaching them to harness the breezes of His power and sail with God?

...Correctable

True discipleship involves some straight conversations. "Iron sharpens iron", but soft, PC, marshmallow conversations rarely change anyone deeply! Our society is so hooked on approval that often we don't know what correction or discipline looks like any more, so we call it rejection. But correction is not rejection, it is protection. And discipline is not disapproval, it's the removal of stuff that is going to harm you!

"God disciplines those He loves" (Hebrews 12:4-11)

Are we raising disciples who will embrace correction and find life in it?

...Connectable

Jesus called His disciples "to be with him". Friendship with a more experienced man or woman of God and a group of fellow disciples is a vital part of healthy growth. Are we allowing a few to get close, to walk the walk with us, and not just listen on Sundays? You can't be connected to everyone, but we all can disciple a few.

...Sendable

Another new word! Jesus "sent them out". Are we sending the troops somewhere, adventuring selflessly as part of a vision bigger than ourselves? Every true disciple is a missionary.

So are we raising disciples or gathering members? Some of us need to change the polarity of our relationship with our church members, because it should not be the leaders who are chasing around after members. Instead, the leaders should be saying to others, *"Follow me, and I will make you..."* (Matthew 4:19).

Leaders of the Church of the future won't simply be carers and counsellors (though both are necessary), but pioneers who get a vision, make it plain for all to see, then march off to a brave new world with disciples following. In this way the Church will become more of a movement than a hospital. An army on the front line, not cadets locked in their barracks!

7. A Revival of Prayer

"The one concern of the devil is to keep Christians from praying. He fears nothing from prayerless studies, prayerless work and prayerless religion. He laughs at our toil, mocks at our wisdom, but trembles when we pray."
Samuel Chadwick

I read recently that "60% of UK churches no longer have a corporate prayer meeting."

Is it possible for a contemporary church to embrace the ancient path of prayer in a way that's relevant, fruitful and "flake free"? Can we adjust our expectation, our models, our enjoyment of it all? Is it actually possible to have a vibrant church community without somehow solving the "Prayer Problem"?

Invigorating prayer is a vital component of a church walking in the fullness of God's presence. Of course, you don't have to call it "the prayer meeting", and there are many ways to do this, but one way or another we must be on fire with prayer for us to host God's glory on the earth.

Let me share 10 things about corporate prayer that I hope will help your church journey:

1. We Can't Live Without It!

Firstly, we've got to admit, hard or not, well attended or failing, busy with outreach or not – we cannot live without prayer in our churches. That's my starting point. Jesus flung tables around with untameable zeal, angry that His House should be anything other than a *"House of Prayer for all nations"* (Matthew 21:13).

Yonggi Cho and countless other revivalists state that, "Prayer is the key to revival" (it's not the whole room though, just the key to the door). The early Church, *"devoted themselves to prayer"* day after day (Acts 2:42). So I have to start from the assumption that all of heaven wants me to solve the lack of passion for prayer in my church or in my own life.

2. Honestly, I Don't Like Praying

To solve the prayer problem, I first have to admit that my flesh really does not like prayer. I do not like getting up early, praying at night, fasting, praying in tongues for an hour or more or stirring up passion. "Jarrod does not like to pray" is something I have to admit in order to "crucify Jarrod" and start living a godly life.

Finding God's passion where mine runs out is vital in so many areas of life! And the church I lead is just as likely to find prayer difficult. Admitting this is a great starting point. God's grace is available in ocean-loads where weakness is admitted.

3. Prayer is a Muscle

So here's my third point. I may not like prayer "in my flesh" but it is a muscle I can develop, with the Spirit's help, until it becomes second nature to pray! After a recent all-night session of prayer in our church, I literally could not stop speaking in tongues. Having prayed in tongues for 12 hours, my prayer muscles learned to operate with greater ease! This is a great truth: *the more I pray, the more I will want to pray!*

4. Smaller, Does Not Mean Irrelevant

In our success-driven age, sometimes I wonder if the small, comparatively poorly attended prayer meeting gets dropped, because it's not seen as successful. It seems like a lot of effort, and generates few headlines. I realise we are doing well if 20% of our church attend a weekly prayer meeting, but is that reason to drop it? I have had to adjust my expectations, overcome my frustration, and relax about prayer meeting attendance. Stop counting heads – start enjoying prayer!

5. Fruitful Prayer

Of course, we get discouraged about prayer unless we can connect it to results and get those headlines! *Intimacy* is the first reason for prayer, but RESULTS has to come a close second! Testimony boards, blogs, social media updates, praise reports and historical journaling is a MUST to retain energy for prayer.

6. A Prayerless Generation

The danger of not delighting in corporate prayer is that

an entire generation of believers will never touch the true depths of intercession, tongues and groanings in the Spirit. A generation who love Jesus must model their lives on Him, who continually *"offered up prayers with loud cries and tears"* (Hebrews 5:7) and was to be found on the mountain of prayer regularly.

7. The Call to Prayer

Most churches experience an ebb and flow in prayer meeting attendance. There seems to be no other church dynamic that requires a regular "Call to..." like prayer. Whenever we "push" prayer, the meetings fill up again and passion is re-ignited. Accepting this dynamic seems to be a part of relaxing into the seasonal nature of prayer in any church.

8. Create Adventures

One great way to call the church to prayer is to highlight significant seasons of prayer. E.g. A 6-week or 21-day fast (where each member picks a day each week to fast); an all-night prayer service; 24 hours of worship; 7 days of listening etc.

Each time we call our congregations to prayer, we flex and grow the muscles of the giant of prayer in our midst. Do it often. Do it creatively.

9. Worship is Prayer

Okay, this is not literally theologically correct, but putting music alongside our prayer is powerful. Mixing prayer and worship makes it incredibly palatable and enjoyable. Flowing prophetically between the two gives it such life.

To pray for hours and get many to enjoy it, blend together worship, prophecy and prayer.

10. Prayer Releases Deeper Worship

I have always said that if a church knows how to pray, you will never need to teach them how to worship. If you want dynamic, vibrant, presence-filled worship in your church, don't teach the people how to worship, teach them how to pray.

* * *

As a pastor, I do not exist to get people into church but into Christ. Getting people to church is easy: put on a youth club, improve your music, run attractional events. But I know that my role is to take that crowd and get some of them into JESUS. That is where lives are truly transformed. It is in encountering Jesus, face to face, that I have been transformed. 9 times out of 10, this has been in prayer, not at a Sunday service or a conference.

Let's take this generation up the mountain of prayer. Britain will never be the same again if we do.

8. A Revival of Atmosphere

"Expectancy is the atmosphere for miracles."
Edwin Louis Cole

I have come to believe that how a church "feels" is more important to it's family than the mechanics of how it operates. In today's lonely, disconnected society, "atmosphere" is everything. People join churches not because the welcome system is perfect, but because the place FEELS right!

You know how, when you're having a conversation with someone, they seem to tick all the boxes you'd look for in a friendship, but they make you feel a little uncomfortable, like something's not quite right? Perhaps you can't quite put your finger on it, but because of it, you know you're never going to glue yourself to that person. It just doesn't feel right. The same is true of church. Most seekers become members intuitively, not because of logical reasoning.

I have found that four key atmosphere's pervade true, successful churches:

1. Energy

All great churches have energy. This is supplied by vision and visionaries. The Great Commission is the vision above all visions, and in varying ways we express it to release focus and goal setting, to draw people to a common cause. There are no passengers (unless you're healing for a while). Everyone wants in on the team and are getting sore elbows fighting for the chance to out-serve each other!

The energy of vision makes mole-hills out of mountains, makes a warrior out of a worrier, a team-member out of the shy-bound soul. We breathe deeper when we inhale vision and all our muscles function better.

What's your vision? Where are you going? What are the prophecies that you're running with? Who are the visionaries on your team? Get vision flowing and it will create a great atmosphere of excitement.

2. Warmth

The second atmosphere of a great church is warmth. The wide embrace of a loving culture. This only comes from a full and unflinching knowledge of God's Grace.

The Pharisees were offended at Jesus (see Luke 15) for the simple reason that He welcomed sinners. Just to nail home His example to them, He spends a lot of time in this chapter saying, "Too right I do! If you're a Lost Sheep I'm going to hunt you down and carry you; if you're a Lost Coin I'll put everything on pause to find you; if you're a Lost Son I'm going to run full pelt at you, throw my arms around you and hug the sin and shame right out of you."

God's kindness will take us places, and make us people, that brow beating never could (Romans 2:4).

While never celebrating sin, every great church has a warm embrace of grace for every faltering sinner, reserving it's harshest authoritarianism for dealing with the self-righteous, self-appointed "Sin-Police" (That's how Jesus did it!). Like Paul in Galatians, we should be so enamoured with God's free gift of grace that we invite controversy and sharp intakes of breath from those who still secretly mutter as though our great salvation was a moral-improvement program, not a love affair in the making. Grace is an enabling from God to overcome our failings by an act of restorative and empowering mercy, dangerously and repeatedly supplied in life-changing quantities.

Is grace at work in your church culture, and more importantly, your own heart? Are you trapped by legalism or do you embrace sinners easily? Is your church leadership style focused on punishing people or restoring people?

Can we create a culture where love covers over a multitude of sins, while also never flinching from the utter holy standards of our God?

3. Honour

Great churches are awash with honour and you can feel it. The chief source of this comes not from hen-pecked followers, but from leaders who know how to be fathers.

The father hearted leader deals not in envy, competition or law making, but in grace, opportunity and making his piece of God's garden a field of dreams for his flock. Honour should be seasoned with good humour and never based on insecure flattery, but rather a spirit of cooperation.

"Honour your Fathers and Mothers and you'll live LONG in the land of Promise!" (Exodus 20:12 paraphrase) is a mind set that creates an atmosphere – and that atmosphere is what "family" is supposed to feel like. Every soul finds that attractive.

Is your culture one that concentrates on the true, godly value of a person, their gifting, their hopes and dreams? Or are you doing church in a culture of sarcasm, fault finding and shame? Let's celebrate the wonder of what God has given us all, concentrating on the grace gift of the divinity in us all, not the humanity where we fall.

4. Presence

Finally, I have found that great churches are electrified with a supernatural sense of the divine presence. God *is* Atmosphere with a Capital "A"!

The source of such an atmosphere is not simply song singing, but an intimacy with the Holy Spirit that can be found in worship, then outworked in our lifestyles, the methodology of church gatherings, and governance, as we seek to grieve-not the One for whom Church exists (Ephesians 2:22).

From Genesis to Revelation God desires to walk and dwell with man in some form of "heaven on earth" kingdom, and the evidence of the arrival of that kingdom has always been the overthrow of the restraints of lower human experience in favour of heaven's culture. Miracles, signs, wonders, healings and the Spirit's communication through prophecy and wisdom flow naturally where heaven is touching earth. (Matthew 6:10.) The lack of such a glory has always been considered a thing of "curse" or punishment.

* * *

The evidence of true kingdom arrival in a church is *power,*

72

not simply talk (1 Corinthians 4:20). *"Is he the One?"* John the Baptist asked in Luke 7:18. Jesus replied, *"...the blind see, the lame walk, the deaf hear, the dead are raised."* The signs of His authenticity were miracles – just as the signs of apostleship are miracles (2 Corinthians 12:12) and the signs accompanying every fresh move of God throughout Church history have been miracles, the overthrow of human laws by heaven's arrival! We are not supposed to simply talk heaven, but DO heaven!

In Acts 4:30 the early Church's response to persecution was not to make themselves more culturally relevant or re-analyse their style (though all that is GOOD!), but rather to passionately cry out to God: *"Stretch forth your hand to perform signs and wonders"* in expectation of a fresh wave of *"power from on high"*. They did not call for a better worship leader to perform, but rather called for God to take centre stage and perform the divine dance of the Creator rejoicing in the midst of the created!

The Energy of Vision. The Warmth of Grace. The Honour of Spiritual Fathers, Mothers, Sons and Daughters. The Presence of God. Combined, these streams of atmosphere create a mighty river, where members and seekers alike are both fearful, in awe, yet deeply attracted to knowing our Heavenly Father through the setting of His earthy family. They become a part of the body.

Finally, read this and dream about it being your church's atmosphere...

"The apostles performed many miraculous signs and wonders among the people. And all the believers used to meet together in Solomon's Colonnade. No one else dared join them, even though they were highly regarded by the

people. Nevertheless, more and more men and women believed in the Lord and were added to their number. As a result, people brought the sick into the streets and laid them on beds and mats so that at least Peter's shadow might fall on some of them as he passed by. Crowds gathered also from the towns around Jerusalem, bringing their sick and those tormented by evil spirits, and all of them were healed." (Acts 5:12-16 NIVUK)

9. A Revival
of Eccentricity

*"Do not fear to be eccentric in opinion, for every opinion
now accepted was once eccentric."*
Bertrand Russell

The Western Church has become too nice. Too measured.
Too tidy.

In recent times I have studied what the greatest 1% of
remarkable churches are doing around the world, and this
is what I've found: every one of them is a little eccentric.

Now, I suppose we each appear a bit eccentric to
someone, but as I have had the privilege of being present in
some of these churches, you really do get a sense that the
leaders and the church families are "unconventional and
slightly strange" – which is the definition of eccentric. They
are also "deviating from regular practice" (an alternative
definition) in several key areas and it is these that I want to
share with you.

Without a doubt, there is an eccentric revolution going
on around the world, with fresh, innovative, daring, fast-

growing churches. I want to present to you the challenge it has brought to me.

Culture: By Design or Default

Kevin Gerald talks about culture always being present in a church, whether by design or default. We certainly do not want a *default* culture in our churches, present simply because of unchecked attitudes, fears, the spirit of the age or the culture of our city or region. What we want is to choose and develop our culture on purpose, by listening to God, through study and with careful thought. So here are several eccentric traits that seem to have been designed purposefully into the cultures of outstanding churches in our nation.

1. Eccentric Positivity

I find great churches today are almost eccentrically positive. Their language, posture, sense of hope and excitement about their mission is unusually upbeat! They love their church eccentrically. They enjoy ministry eccentrically.

Philippians 4 says that we should think about things that are *"true, noble, admirable, trustworthy"* and it would seem these churches have made a choice to be something uncharacteristic in our modern, western society. They choose to be impossibly positive, about everything, concentrating on the admirable and excellent, rather than the failings or the "works in progress".

At a wedding, when the bride walks in, even if you think she's not too hot, her hair's a mess and she isn't that pretty, you would not go to the groom and whisper "Mate, she's a bit of a dog!" would you? Likewise, whenever we criticise, downplay, fault find and nit pick over the imperfections in our church, we are saying to Jesus, the groom, "Your bride simply isn't that hot!" It should not be done.

Eccentric positivity goes that one step too far. In other words, it ventures into the God-realm of faith where we "call things that are not as though they were". This releases energy, excitement, passion and joy in the house of God. Of course, real issues have to be dealt with, and our heads should not be in the sand, but 99 times out of 100, I have found that a positive approach is the very best approach to improvement.

2. Eccentric Honour

The second trait of successful churches is an eccentric level of honour – for their leaders, for their city authorities and, even more unusually, for each other.

I'll be honest, the first time that I sat in a meeting where, as the speaker got up, rather than the obligatory polite hand clap, a full blown standing ovation developed, I thought it was ... well, eccentric! It was over the top. I didn't even know the guy, but peer pressure had me on my feet, clapping along with everyone else.

But as eccentric honour becomes a more comfortable coat to wear, I find that it really does release something when we honour not just our preachers, but we create a culture of honour that runs throughout the house.

Honour creates a culture of cooperation. Have you ever tried to lead a dishonouring teenager anywhere? Or turn a corner of purpose with a team that does not honour your leadership? The only route forward is via rules and enforcement. Never a fun way to lead.

But honour creates cooperation, which in turn releases energy and drive, and injects fun and joy into the journey. It feels like heaven!

It's been said that "flexibility is the barometer of submission". Develop honour among yourselves. Serve each other, obey each other. The sense and power of "team" will be heightened.

3. Eccentric Generosity

In Mark 10:29 Jesus states, *"Those who sell houses, give up families, fields ... for me, will be rewarded."* Without a doubt, impacting our nation deeply in the coming years is going to be very expensive! We will need buildings, schools, social action, staff, multiple congregations, missionaries ... this is a very expensive journey!

And the 1% top flight churches will all have an eccentric level of generosity in their families. We are talking about people selling homes, giving up savings, re-mortgaging homes, taking out loans, giving up holidays – all to invest in something truly eternal. You simply do not get to the top flight of church impact without the culture that Jesus demands of us.

Conversely, a poverty mind set creates a spirit of entitlement. We are in the "Benefit Age" in Great Britain, where everyone thinks they are owed stuff. That can bleed into church life too, making us consumers instead of servants of God. But God would say to those who don't give, *"Would a man rob God?"* (Malachi 3:8). Big, meaty, challenging words. As we learn to live an open handed life towards others and to God Himself, God will live open-handedly towards us – and God's got BIG hands!

4. Eccentric Sound

Top 1% churches all have a unique sound. Many write their own songs. But whether they do or not, there is a well of creativity that expresses the heart of the house.

We need to keep finding the current sound of the season for the house we are in, and let it loose!

"Sing a new song to the Lord" the Bible exhorts. In the coming moves of God, creativity and songs will flow like raging rivers, and worship will become a greater evangelism tool than we ever dreamed. So let the creativity and ideas flow. You'll never be more like God than when you're being creative!

5. Eccentrically Friendly

Another eccentric trait of the top 1% church is their friendliness. They are all irrepressibly warm, hospitable, and it is impossible to get through a service without making half a dozen friends, before, after, even during the service!

They have discovered that the great epidemic of loneliness in our world is something that we the Church can change. Devotion to one another was a hallmark of the early Church (as are all of these eccentric traits), and it is fast becoming one of the great hallmarks of today's greatest churches.

Nobody wants to go to a "friendly" church, they just want friends. And there is a vast difference between putting together a welcome team and developing a culture of truly loving people, eccentrically practicing hospitality. People know the difference between a hosting job and a genuinely warm person who is interested in them as a person.

6. Eccentrically Clean

Finally, I have found, almost without exception, that the world's great churches are places of spiritual health and cleanliness.

David Shearman says, "Healthy churches do not have lumpy carpets." In other words, nothing gets hidden, swept under the rug, or ignored. If you do hide stuff under the carpets, you'll only trip on it later. We've got to deal with issues.

In eccentrically clean churches there is good discipleship, issues of moral sin, gossip and slander are confronted and dealt with in grace, and with a sense of protection for the health of the house.

Old Testament stories of sin in the camp affecting the success and influence of the nation are a stark warning of sin left in the fringes of our membership. Sometimes I wonder if the whole concept of membership needs to be re-evaluated, so that it comes with a greater sense of accountability, since there can be serious repercussions to our sense of favour.

Can someone write anything they please about their church, or a leader, on a social media site, and still expect to be in membership? Is the smell of immorality okay? Are girlfriends and boyfriends behaving as Christians? Is exaggeration and lying acceptable among leaders? In our age of grace, are we still tackling issues of conduct properly?

It is time then, in this day, to revive the eccentric. It is time to become extreme. Extremely positive, exceedingly honouring, gushingly generous, ridiculously friendly, uniquely individual in our sound, unswervingly rigorous in our cleanliness. If we do take these truths, and others, and journey with them to a greater, more exaggerated place than ever before, maybe we'll start to walk as Jesus walked, and see the same effect on our world. Jesus didn't live by half measures. He was, after all, eccentric.

10. A Revival of the Prophetic

"Do not scoff at prophecies."
(1 Thessalonians 5:20 NLT)

Along with any fresh surge of the Spirit through a church will come a fresh rise of the prophetic. It is as inevitable as fire creating heat.

In the Bible there were seasons of dullness towards the voice and visions of heaven; seasons when, *"The word of the Lord was rare."* Allow me to stir some thoughts about the rise of a fresh awakening of the prophetic.

Some Said it Thundered

"'Now my soul is troubled, and what shall I say? "Father, save me from this hour"? No, it was for this very reason I came to this hour. Father, glorify your name!' Then a voice came from heaven, 'I have glorified it, and will glorify it again.' The crowd that was there and heard it said it had thundered; others said an angel had spoken to him. Jesus said, 'This voice was for your benefit, not mine.'"

(John 12:27-30)

In the book of John, God spoke from the heavens and there were three responses from those around:

1. Jesus clearly heard the voice of God
2. Others said they thought they heard an angel i.e. something supernatural
3. Others said it was just thunder, a natural occurrence

Of course, it was in fact God.

It is interesting to note that a group of people, gathered in a single place, having the same spiritual experience, can come up with radically different conclusions. Scary!

I wonder how often God sends a prophetic sign to catch my attention, to emphasise an important truth, relationship or direction? And I wonder at which level my spiritual senses are attuned? Do I see it for what it is? Or am I so dull that I just don't realise it's God communicating at all?

"It's just the weather ... it's a coincidence ... it's unimportant..." I might think. "Too much pizza again, giving me dreams!"

Sometimes I sense it's spiritual, but I'm clueless as to it's meaning. Occasionally I think I catch it, I see it, I get it.

Sometimes the contemporary Church ridicules the prophetic or even considers it theologically incorrect that God speaks to us today, the same way He did in the Bible. There is a danger in labelling anything prophetic as flaky, rather than seeking to work towards a healthy, mature expression of the prophetic in our midst.

I understand: sometimes it's hard to spot the genuine thing, isn't it? Has God actually spoke to me, or am I just making stuff up? The British, especially, have an admirable desire to be real and authentic. Unfortunately, it can also make us unbelieving and even cynical, myself included. So help me out here...

Is God Speaking?

One Sunday we shared plans for an exciting new phase of building in our church. In a significant response, the vast majority of the church gathered at the front of our hall to express solidarity in our journey. One of our girls had broken her foot two weeks before, and could not walk without crutches and great pain. As she walked forward to express her unity, all the pain left her foot and she was spontaneously healed. She hadn't even prayed about it!

So, is that a sign? A prophetic message? Is our walk together as a church being healed and strengthened? Was God putting His seal of approval on our journey and direction? Or was it just God loving Ruth and healing her? Or both?

I know that believers in ancient times would have seen this as heaven's endorsement; a reason to fear the Lord. Perhaps our sophistication has sadly led us beyond that?

In a recent conversation a friend spoke of a vine in his garden that had produced no fruit for years. He cared for it, pruned it, fed it, year by year. It was hopeless. To him it became a spiritual lesson in God's patience with us. A point of learning in his life, wider than the pursuit of grapes!

Then, this year, with a significant spiritual shift having taken place in his life, the vine suddenly burst into life. It's now so fruitful that he's making wine from it! Is that God speaking?

I know prophecy is so much more than hearing God and

repeating what He says, but I am so often dull to it all.

Do you, like me, sense ridicule or open objection from some quarters of the wider Church to such prophetic things – as if the pursuit of such phenomena is immature at best and wacky at worst? We have to ask ourselves though: since when has God ever given us permission to keep the prophetic tidy, culturally acceptable and inoffensive? Could we be missing the very voice of God by such a cynical aversion to the unusual ways of the prophetic?

Natural Disasters

In 1988, when I first came to Hull, God spoke to me of revival in our region using the language of a flood engulfing the area. In 2007 I moved house to where we are now, planting a new church congregation. THE DAY we moved here, there was a flood that struck thousands of homes. All our neighbours were flooded, (though thankfully we were spared. The waters lapped at our door posts as praying congregation members quoted Psalm 91!)

Since 2007 there has been a remarkable shift in our church's desire to reach the lost and see revival; to plant churches and express the Gospel across our region. Was that flood a sign? I certainly think so. It was like a trumpet blast in my ears that said "I told you in 1988, now in 2007 it's starting!"

What Do You See?

"The word of the LORD came to me: 'What do you see, Jeremiah?' 'I see the branch of an almond tree,' I replied. The LORD said to me, 'You have seen correctly, for I am watching to see that my word is fulfilled.'" (Jeremiah 1:11-12)

God questioned the prophets, like Jeremiah, repeatedly, asking *"What do you see?"* as if an eye test was a requirement for ministry and life.

Similarly, Jesus spoke to, *"Those who have ears to hear"* (Mathew 11:15).

In Mark 8:17-18 He says, *"Do you still not see or understand? Are your hearts hardened? Do you have eyes but fail to see, and ears but fail to hear?"*

It would appear that accurately seeing and sensitively hearing is a big deal to God. But are we hardening ourselves to the prophetic and simply humanising the Church and how she is led? Are we placing leadership skills above being Spirit-led? Are we in danger of pushing God out of His own Church because we don't like how He speaks?

Would we even see or hear some of the prophetic instructions of the Bible today? And if we did, could we happily incorporate them into our church styles and services?

Think about Ezekiel, John the Baptist or even Jesus Himself. These are guys you'd actually think twice about inviting to church if you were to study their methods!

And so a rise in the prophetic is going to mean a rise in the unusual. We will need to be prepared for that. In the following chapter, let me show you what I mean...

11. A Revival of the Unusual

"Some, however, made fun of them and said, 'They have had too much wine.'"
(Acts 2:13)

As a guest speaker I turned up to minister at some meetings. On the first night someone came with a bottle of oil, walked right up to the front (past those supposedly "guarding me") and proceeded to pour it over all my head! I was not too chuffed! I ended up in the loos trying to get the oil out of my hair!

The second night, as I walked into the hall the worship had already started. Halfway down the aisle I heard a scream and someone ran at me and launched themselves onto the floor, fully prostrate in front of me. Embarrassed I stepped over them and continued to the front. Later on, whilst I tried to preach, they kept calling out "I need Jesus!" I could barely preach!

The third night another weird thing happened. When I was getting ready to leave, I couldn't find my coat. The next day I learned that someone had nicked it, convinced they would be healed if they wore it!

The strangest thing is, by day four I joined in the madness. After I preached and people had gathered to receive prayer for healing, I felt the Spirit of God say to blow on people's faces! I did this and, to my amazement, the power of God poured out upon them. The very last person to be prayed for was deaf. I felt God say to spit on them. I got the band to play a loud song while I argued with God about this! Finally, I gave in, spat on them, stuck my fingers in their ears and let out an almighty groan! Their ears opened!

Okay, I have a confession to make. None of the above happened to me. Most of it never has. But it did ALL happen to JESUS and the early disciples!!!

Jesus Was Unusual

When the Spirit begins moving in your church, you will find the anti-flake brigade becomes very vocal. Every time God does something prophetic and unusual, any time anyone shows more passion than is considered "appropriate", they brand people flakes. It is the defence mechanism of Tidy Church. It is the rage of humanism in the Church today, seeking to limit a mighty God to tidy, containable, comprehensible works.

I completely understand why people worry about attention seekers, people with issues who seem to continually desire the weird side of prophecy, "out there" worship and the supernatural. I understand that when God does something once, we should not make an entire culture out of it. People who are attention seekers for all the wrong reasons should be corrected.

But can I also be really honest?

The Bible is FULL of weird stuff. To want Jesus, but not want the unusual, supernatural, culture of heaven, is like asking to swim but not get wet! And when we teach our young people, by our example, to brand as "flaky" anything we don't understand, we are teaching them to undermine a vast portion of valid, scriptural activity. More troubling still, we grieve the Holy Spirit.

If You Want Fruit, You'll Need a Little Nut

I have discovered that, sometimes to get fruit you need a little nut.

It took a nut (Joshua) to shout at Jericho's walls. They would still be standing if the people had not shouted!

It took a nut (Moses) to lift a walking stick over a sea, expecting it to part.

It took a nut (Namaan) to wash in the Jordan seven times in order to be healed.

It took a nut (Ezekiel) to lie on his side for months on end as a prophetic sign to the nation.

Another nut (Elijah) stuck his head between his knees in prayer and, under a virtually cloudless, sky said, "I hear the sound of heavy rain!"

It took a nut (Noah) to build a boat on dry land to save animals from floods caused by rain, when it had never rained.

The early disciples were so nutty that on the day of Pentecost people were bewildered, perplexed and made fun of them! (Yet, 3,000 still got saved in this atmosphere!)

A nut pushed through the crowd to touch Jesus' garment. A nut cried out, *"Son of David, have mercy on me!"* while all the religious folk told blind Bartimaeus to calm down! A nut called Zacchaeus climbed a tree and Jesus came to his house.

And Jesus Himself was the *most* unusual. He spat on people during prayer, groaned loudly, sighed and cried in prayer. He allowed women to weep over His feet, pour oil and perfume on Him and wipe His feet with their hair. He would disappear off into the mountains unannounced, walk on water, turn a fish into an ATM and make mud packs to put on people's eyes. He also preached the wildest, most confusing, story-laden sermons ... on purpose! He loved sinners and scolded the religious.

In other words, our heroes from the pages of Scripture modelled lives that were unusual, eccentric and counter-cultural. This is what must happen if we are going to live in the centre of God's destiny for our lives.

So before you brand everything that is prophetic as flaky, you must be aware that you may just be rejecting the childlike kingdom of heaven! Rejecting the Bible! We must stop branding the unusual as something that was acceptable only in days past, for the long dead heroes of Church history. Some ministers today would not like Wigglesworth, Wesley, Finney, Elijah, Ezekiel or even Jesus, if they ministered at their churches for a weekend!

I have staff who have spat on people and they've been healed. I have known the Spirit cause me to run as miracles flowed and seen God's glory impact streets outside our church buildings.

I have received direct prophecy through the television and cried out in American Indian song (well, that's what it sounded like!) at an open vision of needy children (our church is now involved in educating, feeding and bringing the Gospel to over 1500 of these children a week!)

That's Not Flaky, It's Kingdom

Jesus told us to "go" and I think we're all agreed on that. But some aren't so sure about the "signs of the kingdom" He said would follow, worried about those they fear may just be acting weird for the sake of it. As ever, the answer to misuse is not disuse, but correct use. We simply cannot stop unusual things from happening in our churches, because in so doing we will throw the baby out with the bath water; the kingdom out with the unusual.

Wesley and Wonders

Let me pause before anyone thing thinks I am suggesting we should simply let wild, unbridled wackiness fill our churches and call it a move of God. Nothing could be further from my heart. But I do know this: if we try to tidy up church and keep everything under control, we will inevitably lock God out.

In Mike Bickle's report, *The Manifestations of the Spirit in Church History*, he writes:

"John Wesley, the founder of the Methodist movement, was the most well-known revival preacher of his time. He reported that 'people dropped on every side as thunderstruck as they fell to the ground, others with convulsions exceeding all description and many reported seeing visions. Some shook like a cloth in the wind, others roared and screamed or fell down with involuntary laughter.'"

John Wesley's prayerful take on the unusual things that

happened around him as he led the nation into a place of revival over several decades was this:

"Lord send us revival without its defects, but if this is not possible, send revival, defects and all."

In other words, if we desire God to move, let us not be surprised that we get both unusual things sent by heaven, but also human mistakes, errors, extremes or, as Wesley puts, it "defects". Better to have a little unusual activity going on, rather than have no move of the Spirit at all.

We do not exist to sanitise God for the masses. Let us allow Him to move and teach (even correct) those who go to fleshly extremes. But let us not try to remove the unusual Might and Mystery of our God.

Will He Touch Us Too?

I remember leading a service in a sports facility in the middle of a community where we were planting a church. I had not planned it, but the meeting became very powerful at one point. Many fell to the floor, deliverances were taking place, some were crying, many were in the throes of deep intercession. None of us looked too cool, but it was very powerful.

It was some time well into the service when I realised that we had forgotten to pull the curtains down one side of the hall and a large group of teenage lads were staring at us all through the floor to ceiling windows, a look of utter incredulity on their faces!

One of our lads went out to chat to them. "What on earth is going on in there?!" they asked, with a few swear words thrown in that I won't repeat.

"God is touching people lives," our guy answered.

Listen to the response of an average, un-churched teenager in Britain today:

"Wow! Do you think He'd touch us too?"

You see, the world doesn't want more religion, or tidier religion. They are asking "Is there a God?" Can we give them God in all His glory and power?

Another time, one of our lads was trying to share the gospel with some teenage lads near our main church building. Noticing one had a bad leg he said, "Can I pray for your leg and if God heals you, can I talk to you all about Jesus?"

Before they could think about it, he prayed, and the lad with a bad leg was healed, shaking his leg around and saying "I can feel something in me!"

"It's just God!" our guy said, as the lad started to feel God's presence.

"Can we feel Him?" his friends asked, and within minutes, a row of teenage lads, rough as can be, lined up on a street in Hull, put their hands out to be prayed for and began to shake under God's power. By that night many had given their lives to Christ.

Over-Sensitive

I sometimes wonder if we harbour the same attitude towards God's ways as teenage sons do to their fathers: they love their dads, but they find their ways slightly embarrassing. God is not "with-it" because He doesn't respect cultural boundaries. He is confident, expressive. To our tiny minds He seems to act "unusually". So perhaps we're slightly embarrassed by Him?

But like most teenagers, are we being OVER-sensitive in

our embarrassment of God's unusual ways, thinking that our friends will think our Dad is a bit weird? When actually, to continue the analogy, our "unsaved" teenage friends will think He's really cool, just as He is!

You see, I have found that most non-Christians are perfectly happy with God moving unusually, as long as it's maturely done, explained, servant hearted and caring – not attention seeking or manipulative.

Some of my team have laid hands on people in the street, leading to healing, prophecy and ultimately salvation. Others have anointed people with oil in the streets and seen healings take place. Many, many non-Christians have fallen to the floor overwhelmed by God's power, then got up asking what happened and got saved! Others have prophesied about leadership and ministry to people who weren't even saved – but the non-Christian simply responded, "Well I'd better get right with God then!" Words of knowledge have flowed in open air services and non-Christians have responded, getting healed and leaving behind hearing aids, walking aids, crutches and limb supports.

That's our God!

He may be unusual at times, but we can't change that. Not if we're going to be Bible-believing people.

A Peculiar People

"But ye are a chosen generation, a royal priesthood, an holy nation, a peculiar people." (1 Peter 2:9)

The kingdom IS unusual. YOU are supposed to be peculiar (at least slightly!) God is not English, polite or politically correct. So we in the UK tread a difficult balance between being cultural sensitive to both heaven and our Western culture!

To conclude, I believe, through reading the Bible and through my experience of 25 years of miracles, salvations and prophecy...

...You can't actually have kingdom fruit without a little nut every now and then.

12. A Revival
of Church Growth (Part 1)

"The longer a church exists, the more concerned members become with self-preservation ... and the less concerned with the church's original reason for being."
Source unknown.

One of my greatest frustrations with the Church in the UK, is the lack of presence-orientated churches that grow beyond 250 in membership. Many don't make it past 70.

I suppose I must define presence-orientated again. To me this speaks of churches where there is a general expectation for the moving of the Spirit beyond song singing and preaching in a service, and in the day to day life of church members. They are places where the Spirit can literally have His way.

Unfortunately, many of these churches are smaller in size, so the obvious conclusion might be that a passion for the things of the Spirit is detrimental to church growth. This then leads to a general lack of influence, because no matter which way you cut it, success brings influence. It is human nature to desire success.

But I believe this can be overcome. I believe most Spirit-orientated churches are not small because they love the presence, but because they usually lack other ingredients that bring growth.

In our church, we have consistently aimed for a culture where the Spirit can move, He is not restricted, prophecy, miracles, moves of God, touches of Pentecost abound, and yet we consistently seek to build an environment of growth.

Seekers Love the Spirit

Firstly, I can tell you that presence churches – who may have longer meetings, longer preaches, unusual moves of God, the prophetic, healing, people being overwhelmed by God and passionate or loud music – do not in any way put off seekers! There is a generation of people genuinely seeking a God who is real, supernatural (why have any other kind?!) and who are quite willing to enjoy spiritual experiences.

In fact, if their church doesn't provide them, their hunger for spirituality often leads these people into drugs, or to mediums and clairvoyants. We need Spirit-filled, miracle working, growing churches today to fill this hunger for spirituality!

Here are the 9 truths I believe presence churches need to understand to see numerical growth today:

1. Moves of the Spirit Do Not Grow Churches (in the way you might think!)

In and of itself, prayer meetings, people being overwhelmed by the Spirit, accurate prophecies and outstanding miracles do not usually directly grow a church numerically. They are the culture of the kingdom, but not the means by which a church grows in size.

The church grows by constantly GOING FROM the church services to reach the lost, then by discipleship and a lovingly organised family culture. Historically, outpourings of the Spirit that are not accompanied by good organisation eventually leave the church smaller, not bigger, since we must address the issue of the wineskin, not simply the wine. We must develop the container, not just the contents.

2. Organisation and Planning Are Not a Threat to the Spirit

Usually, far from embracing good organisation or (and here's a big one) even good business sense, some leaders of presence-orientated churches shun them as a threat to God's moving. They seem to believe Jesus declaration, *"I will build my Church"* means that all they have to do is lay about on a carpet and prophesy, and somehow it will all happen.

Actually, God makes the church grow like He makes a garden grow. In Eden, the growth was divine but Adam, the man, had to tend it, cultivate it, shape it and prune it. It is when Spirit-filled leaders cultivate their garden, instead of letting it grow wild, that healthy, fruit-giving growth comes.

Phil Pringle states, comparing a church to a garden, "You should have seen this place when God did it all without me. It was a mess!" In other words, God brings growth, but organisation is our delegated role from Him to bring order.

3. Weird is ONLY Wonderful When God's in it!

A brief reading of the book of Acts, and even the gospels,

shows that walking in the supernatural can be quite controversial, strange, weird even! Fires on heads, mud packs, spitting on people, prophetic declarations, miracles, tongues in front of non-believers. In among all this people get saved!

And even though I'm into weird, there is a limit to weird for weird's sake! Some people actually seem to WANT weird, which is worrying. I can cope with weird, but it's NEVER my preference! Keep that weird, "Gotta throw oil, carry a prayer stick and shout all the time" culture in check. Never lose the ability to be all things to all men.

4. Amateur Dramatics Discredit God
Continuing this theme, when operating in the supernatural, we should try to become proficient in the realms of basic supernatural operation by practicing away from our main services. Learn how to pray for healing lovingly or how to prophecy without embarrassing people, without experimenting on poor visitors! Nothing puts people off the supernatural like poor practice. That's not God's fault, it's ours.

5. Tabernacle Syndrome
"About eight days after Jesus said this, he took Peter, John and James with him and went up onto a mountain to pray. As he was praying, the appearance of his face changed, and his clothes became as bright as a flash of lightning. Two men, Moses and Elijah, appeared in glorious splendour, talking with Jesus. They spoke about his departure, which he was about to bring to fulfilment at Jerusalem. Peter and his companions were very sleepy, but when they became

fully awake, they saw his glory and the two men standing with him. As the men were leaving Jesus, Peter said to him, 'Master, it is good for us to be here. Let us put up three shelters—one for you, one for Moses and one for Elijah.' (He did not know what he was saying)." (Luke 9:28-33)

I think that no stream of church struggles with what I call "Tabernacle Syndrome" like presence-orientated churches. If God has moved in the past, we want to put up a tent and stay there, just like Peter on the mountain saying, "It's good to stay here!" But we don't only "stay there" spiritually – it seems that often, the decor of that move, the music, the language, the dress sense, all seems to be "suspended", giving everything about the church a "dated" look.

Beware of getting stuck in an old move of God. Get back down that mountain and get on with living in your era, taking all the goodness of that God-encounter with you.

You live in the 21st Century, so let your church, dress sense and music reflect that. God might look at the heart, but everyone who comes seeking God in your church is going to look at the packaging. Poor packaging turns off the seeker. Get up to date!

6. Deal With Your Prophetic Personality Issues

Lots of presence-orientated churches are led by prophetic personalities (like me!) and one of our weaknesses is an isolationist spirit (just read about Elijah). Prophets love their own company and time alone with God, and yet also become morose, lonesome and unfriendly. Overcome this by pouring yourself into community in your own church, and also by hooking up with some minister friends with very different ministry gifts to you.

If you can lighten up a bit, it will affect your church positively. Church ultimately needs the leadership of all 5 ministries (Ephesians 4:11 says apostle, prophet, evangelist, pastor, teacher) to be fully healthy. You need a 5-cylinder engine to power a healthy, growing church, even if those who compliment you only visit regularly.

7. You Have to Develop Your Leadership Skills

Since presence-orientated leaders see their "Spirit walk" as their main means to success, they often fail to invest in their leadership skills. Look at their bookshelves, their preaches, what conferences they attend, and you will often find very little investment in quality leadership thinking. Read Maxwell and Warren alongside your favourite revivalists and prophetic teachers, and some of those skills will grow.

Enjoying God's presence is a spiritual gift and experience, but growing church is also an engineering job. We need to start looking at church growth material if we want to grow. More about this later.

8. You Can't Build on a Single Value

Though, like me, "presence" might be your greatest value, you cannot build a church on one value. You have a whole Bible, full of the criteria for healthy Christians and churches. Invest in discipleship, leadership training, excellence, community outreach, good music, contemporary venues and caring community structures, and you will grow.

9. Leader, YOU Make Church Grow

John Maxwell says, "everything rises and falls on leadership".

What grows a church? The work of God in the leader. If He's put you in charge as a ruler over God's household, you can do it! Pray for His grace to help you. Study to find good skills. Plan for growth and it will happen! If you TRULY have a passion to reach the lost and grow a great church, then you will lead a growing church.

13. A Revival
of Church Growth (Part 2)

"A church that has no interest at all in increasing its number of converts is, in essence, saying to the rest of the word, 'You all can go to hell.'"
Rick Warren

Once we have decided to work through the issues of tension that come with a church devoted to both Word and Spirit, we will begin to search out ways to break through the glass ceilings of church growth.

In the next two chapters I want to highlight some of the basic changes we've made as a church to release growth, without losing any devotion to the Holy Spirit and His moving.

Firstly, and these are the very basics of church growth, in a Western setting it is said that to grow both numerically and in health, we need the five basics in place and running well, before adding other elements to our church program or activities. Most of these revolve around making your Sundays as great as you possibly can, as you will find these are usually your greatest place of growth. If you can simply turn your visitors into dedicated members you will grow! To do that, the 5 basics to give your attention to are:

1. The Best Possible Worship Experience

The best, most worshipful musicians you can muster, helping to provide an environment where people feel they meet God.

2. The Best Possible Preaching

"Giving everyone a go" on the preaching rota or rustling up a few thoughts in your spare time won't build church. You need to spend time preparing to bring your A-Game in preaching, teaching and ministering to people. Truly feed the sheep by taking preaching seriously, and they will stay.

3. The Best Possible Children's Work

Many visitors are looking for somewhere for their children to grow up having fun and growing in God, and this usually works during the adult's service or at least the teaching time.

4. The Best Possible Youth Work

Having somewhere for teens to grow together in God is another vital aspect for families as they connect into church.

5. A Healthy Small Group Network

Somewhere for people to meet and develop close friendships in an environment other than a Sunday service is vital. This is where your community will grow strong in friendship and trust – absolutely vital when a growing church faces the storms that will come!

The 5 basic activities above are vital for getting church ready to grow. Alongside that there are 5 basic elements to moving the church into that growth in a Western, modern church setting:

1. Commitment to the Commission

Jesus left a divine command ringing in His disciples' ears: Go, Go, Go! Preach, publish, broadcast the good news to all creation and make disciples of them, baptising, healing with signs and wonders (Mark 16:15-18). Though every church mission statement can be slightly different, at the end of the day every department of every church and every person in every pew, must be challenged, inspired, taught and shown how to live a life that fulfils this command.

It must pump like blood through the veins of your church, so that you have a congregation that is a pioneering revolution in progress, not a hospital ward (though every church needs a hospital ward!)

Perhaps one of the greatest distractions to true growth is when we engage in social action as a bridge into our community, thinking that this, in itself, is evangelism. It is essential that we care for the poor, but this in itself doesn't grow the church – often because although we are caring, we're not preaching. Immense amounts of time, energy and money can be spent "doing good" instead of "preaching good". Many churches are distracted making the seats on the bus to hell feel more comfortable, instead of saving souls. If you can, do both. But if you have limited time and resources – save souls!

Don't misunderstand me, our church's ministry involves reaching over 2,000 people a week in care, providing education, food and poverty alleviation. Yet this is small compared to our work to reach the lost with the gospel and is a by-product of our love for people. I regularly ask of our leaders, regarding social action projects, "How may have been saved? How many are disciples? Are we gathering disciples?" In many cases, if something is not successfully reaching souls, it gets shut down.

We must think, breathe, act and spend as if the Great Commission is the greatest thing we do. When we do that, growth occurs.

2. A Bringing Culture

This will result in people bringing people to church. "Bringing" is found all over the gospels, as people brought others to Jesus. From the leader's perspective, there must be loads of events, big or small/attractional or relational, to bring people to. When a church has a bringing culture, quite simply the flow of visitors to your church becomes your greatest source of growth. Don't underestimate it. Every Sunday should be a salvation service!

3. Energy

When a place is alive with vision, energy and momentum, it can't help but be attractive. Places that are energetically positive, bounding from week to week, excited about what God is doing among them – these places grow.

Now you might think, "I wish our church had that!" The truth is, you build it. Leaders create this environment on purpose. They get vision from God, throw the vision at people, and throw people into the vision. Get people working, focused on the Great Commission, working in their skill set areas, celebrating successes and laughing about failures and you will develop a place with energy.

4. Floor Space

This is really practical in the Western setting. Floor space affects your growth!

Someone asked me the other day, "Why isn't my church growing?" I asked how many people came along.

"About 75" was the reply.

"And how big is your hall?" I asked.

"It'll take about 100."

"You're pot bound," I replied. "It won't grow any more. If you are 70-80% full, apart from special events, it is unlikely you'll grow beyond your floor space. You need more meetings or a new hall to grow into."

I studied and discovered this when I first took on our church. If you achieve the first three points to stimulating church growth, this fourth one is the bottleneck that will stop it. You have to keep adding floor space and service times in order to grow.

Apart from the first three points being evident in our church, the main practical decision that has grown our church has been the continued addition of multiple services, multiple venues, extension services and church plants. It is well proven that most growing churches have "multiple" services of some sort, whether in the same venue or in satellite congregations. Nothing has released the pioneering vision for our 90-year old church like pioneering new meetings and churches in different places.

Be brave. Pick a village or town nearby with no church like yours. With the guidance of the Holy Spirit, go and plant an extension service by just booking a hall and putting on worship, speakers and some hospitality. Tell everyone you're coming (one year we put 120,000 fliers through doors and rented 10 billboards!) And pray for people to come!

Get yourself some more floor space and you'll grow. (P.S. Usually a Sunday night service in addition to your Sunday morning is not a "multiple service" in the best sense of church growth. It will often comprise only the really committed people from the morning service, plus a few others. To really push for growth, put on two Sunday morning services, either one after the other, or in two venues. That will create proper space for growth).

5. A Cycle of Life

Once you've got visitors coming to your services, create a net to catch them. This requires something like:

a) Good clear altar calls and response systems. I literally had to lay on my face and ask God to help me with this, as for years I was hopeless at altar calls for salvation. Seek God for ways that work for you.

b) Good follow up and conversation, retaining names and addresses, and giving those who respond Bibles, CDs and teaching aids. Get your best "smilers" on this team and make sure all ages are represented.

c) Develop a way for newcomers to get connected to your church. A course, a welcome meal, a party – anything! Just get them connecting with your leaders and into small groups as quickly as possible.

d) Start a New Believer's Course (e.g. Alpha is fab!), giving people the basics of the Christian faith.

e) Connect people even deeper through small groups and team membership. There are a few things almost anyone can do (even if they're still not saved!) So we try to get people working asap, as it glues them into our family.

f) Pastoral Care: as a church grows, not everyone can connect to the leader or leadership couple and you'll need to develop a "pastoral care team", which I'll talk about in the next chapter. Together you'll create enough relational capacity to grow.

14. A Revival
of Organisation

"Plan ahead. It was not raining when Noah built the ark."
Source Unknown

Once you've decided that you're going to grow and you begin to put in place basic plans and activities similar to those we've looked at, you're going to face a new "good problem". It is this: church gets more complex as it gets bigger (I know, fun right?!)

Possibly one of the most significant papers that has advised the development of our church over the last few years is, *Leadership and Church Size Dynamics – How Strategy Changes with Growth* by Dr Timothy Keller.

One of the great glass ceilings in church growth (and therefore a barrier to the healthy salvation and discipleship of precious people) is a lack of understanding of how numerical size changes the complexities of a church community. Because of numerical size our leadership tools, styles and emphasis have to change as we go through certain sociological size boundaries.

Without a doubt, the dynamics of church change at around the 40, 150, 400 and 800 size thresholds. What gets you to one stage often won't get you to the next. You need to adjust, learn, up-skill and deal with the (different) glass ceilings that hold you back.

This is why many of our churches plateau. We hit an invisible ceiling that only wisdom can fix. I once heard Rick Warren say, "How you lead when you have 25,000 is quite different to when you've got 23,000!" Okay, when I got off the floor laughing (mainly because such numbers are not on my planet!) I realised there was an incredible truth here. Regardless of the numbers involved, there has to come a shift in how we operate as we move through different phases of growth. As a church, we have indeed had to change how we lead, as we have gone through size barriers (though ours was more in the hundreds than the thousands!) So here are some hints and tips on how church changes as we grow and navigate the size barriers.

House Church (up to 40)

This church is essentially a large house group. It's highly relational and everyone can have a powerful say in what goes on, since collaboration is easy and natural – there are only a few people to consult. Communication happens by word of mouth and decisions are made by consensus. The church grows through warm relationships and connections. There is virtually no structure or formal organisation required, other than a lay leader or two. (Sounds like heaven!)

In order to grow, and especially to minister to various groups in a meaningful way (e.g. children and youth), the church must accept it needs to move out of a house or small hall setting and introduce a little structure. Most importantly, the people must collectively decide and choose to grow together to the next stage.

Small Church (40-200)

This is quite a wide category, but it's in this band that the "small church" exists. At this size it can still be highly relational, though not quite as intimate as a house church. People will expect to have lots of face-to-face time and to know the names of all the other congregation members. Lots of personal contact with the leader/leadership couple is expected and they in turn have the time to give themselves personally to a group of this size. The leaders will find themselves becoming stretched to achieve this as the group tops 150+ members.

At the 150-200 stage the church will have to choose to prepare for greater growth or accept that they will plateau.

Changes in this community are processed quite slowly, allowing time for people to adjust, in order to take everyone along. Leadership is still largely "lay leadership" and important influencers within the congregation will help to maintain stability (or otherwise!) The church still grows largely because of relational connections and warmth, since it is still quite a small community where everyone knows each other. As such, entering as a newcomer is easy and informal.

Communication is still largely face to face, via word of mouth, since everyone knows each other. This is a very comfortable size for a church, thus many (most) will remain somewhere in this size bracket. As the church grows, however, the leader will start to feel the need for better administration, a higher calibre of platform ministry (I will explain why later) and try to become more "visionary" in style or gift. Up to now, the leader has acted as shepherd. To enter the next phase he/she will be required to be "visionary".

In order to grow beyond 200 people, one of the major glass ceilings to break through is accepting that we can no longer know everyone's name and we can no longer all relate directly to the senior leaders/leadership couple. At this threshold we face the choice of growing or remaining nice and cosy. Some people will feel threatened by this and start saying things like, "This church is too big ... I don't know everyone ... we are losing the family feel."

Tim Keller points out that, "It is a sociological fact that a full-time minister cannot personally shepherd more than about 150–200 people." Sociologists have also pointed out that a person can only really have meaningful, working friendships with a maximum of 150 people. This is often why church growth stagnates at the 120-150 person level.

Therefore, at this point developing a pastoral care system or appointing further people as pastors is vital. In our church we have lay couples caring for 50-70 people, who regard them as pastors, having been taught that it is impossible for me to be a face-to-face pastor with hundreds of members. As a team, we care deeply for our people, but the team of pastors becomes paramount.

Often hiring a second leader – an assistant pastor, youth pastor or associate – can help this dynamic, providing more "senior leaders" for people to connect to closely.

Teaching, leading and envisioning are required to help people to see the potential of this new place if the community is to accept growing to the next size.

If the meeting hall is becoming full, often one of the easiest way to grow beyond it is to add multiple services or even multiple sites, each of which will bring a growth spurt.

The other change at this size threshold is that the power of leadership becomes less democratic and is more in the hands of the senior team, appointed lay leaders and staff. Thus trust and communication become highly important.

Medium Sized Church (200-450)

At the next size, things like bringing new believers into the heart of a large family becomes something that has to take place in a more organised and deliberate way, whereas before it could happen naturally. A community of 150 people is small enough to embrace newcomers with little organisation, but now it has to be planned and well executed, whilst remaining warm, natural and loving!

At this stage, the wisdom of Jethro begins to be required. Let's look at the biblical account:

"The next day Moses took his seat to serve as judge for the people, and they stood around him from morning till evening. When his father-in-law (Jethro) saw all that Moses was doing for the people, he said, 'What is this you are doing for the people? Why do you alone sit as judge, while all these people stand around you from morning till evening?' Moses answered him, 'Because the people come to me to seek God's will. Whenever they have a dispute, it is brought to me, and I decide between the parties and inform them of God's decrees and instructions.' Moses' father-in-law replied, 'What you are doing is not good. You and these people who come to you will only wear yourselves out. The

work is too heavy for you; you cannot handle it alone. Listen now to me and I will give you some advice, and may God be with you. You must be the people's representative before God and bring their disputes to him. Teach them his decrees and instructions, and show them the way they are to live and how they are to behave. But select capable men from all the people—men who fear God, trustworthy men who hate dishonest gain—and appoint them as officials over thousands, hundreds, fifties and tens. Have them serve as judges for the people at all times, but have them bring every difficult case to you; the simple cases they can decide themselves. That will make your load lighter, because they will share it with you. If you do this and God so commands, you will be able to stand the strain, and all these people will go home satisfied. Moses listened to his father-in-law and did everything he said." (Exodus 18: 13-24)

At above 200, even the leaders start to struggle to know everyone's names and the church needs to develop its leadership structure so that it is made up of many small teams and groupings, each connecting with different leaders and pastors who, in turn, are answerable to the senior leader or senior team. The senior minister then becomes more of a team leader to leaders, rather than a personal pastor to the congregation.

Some of the older members may object to not having the pastor's "ear" as they used to. "He's changed" might be the common complaint! (Actually, he's possibly just much busier than in the early days).

At this point leadership becomes more complex and the leader's capacity that brought this group to the 200 mark will be being stretched (mine were!). At this point, adding to the team more strategic thinkers becomes important (instead of solely preachers and pastors), because now there are issues to think through such as employment plans, finance budgets, compliance laws, building projects, outreaches and training schools.

Whereas a small church is led by a team of people operating mainly in the pastoral gift, now it is usually led by strategic visionaries and planners, who are supported by pastors, who in turn continue to connect more deeply with people in the form of pastoral groups and ministry teams.

Since adjusting senior leadership roles becomes highly important in this season, it is vital that people have a fluid attitude to roles and titles. In the smaller church setting, it's reasonable to think, "I have been given a role, it's mine to do for the next 20 years." In the medium sized church, however, you need people to buy into the vision of the church, not their own role, and to be willing to move around various roles/teams to do what is required.

An aid to retaining this fluidity can be using things like annual reviews to help position people in the appropriate place for the next season. The senior leadership team will have to become more strategic and less pastoral, whilst never losing sight of a love for people and thus creating a harsh organisation.

It must also be said that from the 200-person point onwards, you really have to work at making church feel smaller, while it gets bigger. Suddenly small groups are really important, otherwise people feel lost in the crowd.

In our church we emphasise that we all need to "live in circles, not rows". Rows of people in a church meeting hall singing songs led from the front, is not really a church community. Members must not think that they belong simply because they attend services, because, in fact, true "members" live in circles i.e. they meet in homes, coffee shops, parks and teams, to live life together in small groups.

Rows in a big meeting hall cannot create community, they just celebrate community. Thus, the Sunday service becomes a celebration of a Monday-Saturday life lived out in small groups and teams across a geographic area.

To become bigger, you must become smaller.

The other thing to note at this size is that the quality of the services must improve. In a small church, a bit of out of tune singing is ignored, because everyone knows and likes "sister so and so" and they have a relational connection. This dynamic changes as you grow (and there are more people don't know the "singer"), so people will simply judge the quality of the singing, playing or presentation without that relational history. At this stage of growth poor singing becomes a distraction to worship and ceases to be something sweet to smile about.

It applies to all areas: excellence in worship, preaching, in the flow of the services and communication. They all need to improve at this size because the church is subtly becoming an organisation people have to join, rather than a small family they can wander into.

Large Church (450+)

Tim Keller gives us several points to ponder regarding going beyond the 450 barrier and on in to the thousands. He states,

"The very large church has several traits that attract seekers and young adults in particular:

• **Excellence** – Those with no obligation to go to church based on kinship, tradition, ethnicity, or local history are more likely to attend where the quality of arts, teaching, children's programs and so on is very high

• **Choices** – Contemporary people are used to having options when it comes to the schedule or type of worship, learning, support services and the like

• **Openness to Change** – Generally, newcomers and younger people have a much greater tolerance for the constant changes and fluidity of a large church, while older people, long-term members and families are more desirous of stability

• **Low Pressure** – Seekers are glad to come into a church and not have their presence noticed immediately. The great majority of inquirers and seekers are grateful for the ease with which they can visit a large church without immediately feeling pressured to make a decision or join a group."

So there are some sociological reasons, particularly in Western society, why church may or may not grow. I do hear people object to this thought at times, but usually its from those with smaller churches who want to resist the personal challenge of growth. Personally, I have repeatedly faced the "I'm not sure I'm up to this" thoughts in my own head. But as I've been willing to change, grow, stretch, humble myself before more experienced leaders and get advice, I've found that I can grow and so can the church community I'm honoured to lead. In a sense, it's simple. But that doesn't mean it's easy!

A revival of growth and organisation will be almost as

vital as a revival of the Spirit's power in our churches. One is the wineskin, the other the wine. One is the bones, the other the breath.

Wine in a brittle wineskin will be lost. We must take time to revive our organisation and leadership skills, even if that is personally challenging. There are endless books and blogs we can read and conferences we can attend that will help us in all this. Develop a voracious appetite to learn and you will up-skill in this and many other areas.

Let us seek not just the wine, the oil, the breath and fire of God – let's also seek the Architect, the Builder, the Author and the Wise One. Wisdom will build a house, then glory will fill it. Let's go find that wisdom!

15. Overcoming the Critics

"To avoid criticism, do nothing, say nothing, be nothing."
Elbert Hubbard

As we seek to move forward in intimacy, prayer, apostleship, prophecy, growth, organisation and all the other values a church today should treasure, then we are going to face critics; critics in our own heads, on our church councils and in our congregations. Here is a countdown of 10 of the biggest battles I have worked through as I have sought to move forward in the wisdom of God:

TEN: "Do we really need all these lights and tricks to worship?"

When confronted with a culture beyond our own, we tend to criticise it as a defence mechanism. Things like lighting rigs, certain styles of music, dress, visual effects (whether a stained glass window or lasers), are all just a reflection of culture. We don't need any of it, just like we don't need seats, carpets, a roof, or even clothes to worship. But I would rather you dressed in public and that we gathered out of the rain, and I think God expects us to use every bit of cultural development available to express our worship. Let's let the lighting engineers "Praise him on the lighting desk", without being miserable about it.

NINE: "It's not as good as it was."

Ah! The power of nostalgia. The reality is, "It wasn't as good as it was", either! The human mind is designed to fade away painful or boring periods of life and gold emboss positive experiences. The result is we always give the distant past an unrepeatable perfection in our minds as history concertinas into the good memories. It actually **wasn't** as good as you remember. In God, who leads from glory to glory, your best days are always ahead of you. As they say, even nostalgia is not what it was!

EIGHT: "We miss being together."

Usually aimed at leaders who have taken people into multiple services or venues due to growth. The reality is you were never ALL together before, as 100% of a church's members are very rarely in the building at the same time, even when you run only one service. If souls are God's greatest concern then large amounts of people being discipled is important, and multiple venues and services are a must for the way forward. We must put the Great Commission above cosiness.

SEVEN: "Youngsters weren't like that in my day."

Said by aging believers who may have past their best and perhaps are genuinely disappointed in young people. The truth is, "It isn't YOUR day (of being youthful) anymore", it is today! The pressures are quite different and perhaps sometimes we forget what is was like to work through peer pressures and youthful pride. The last verses of the Old Testament show that, "The hearts of the fathers must turn to the children", not vice versa. It is for the older generation to turn and embrace the young, then they will accept the counsel of the former. Let's do our best to understand the young, then each generation will tell of His works to the next.

SIX: "It's all flesh!"

Said by the quieter Christians of happy clappy believer's gatherings. Well, the snoozy, arms folded, seated worshipper is ALL FLESH too! I'd prefer my flesh "happy and clappy" as scientists have proven it's better for your health! I'd also say of worship, if it's in the book of Psalms, let's do it. God put it there for a reason. Clap, shout, dance, cry out, bang loud cymbals. "Make His praise glorious!"

FIVE: "He's not my style."

Often said of preachers who shout, pace, or tell too many stories. Unfortunately, God does love to face us with problematic style issues. He did in the form of Elijah, John the Baptist and even Jesus. If we met them today, in ministry mode, we would really struggle with their very "un-PC" shouting, fire falling, camel hair clothing, locust meals, repeated messages (John: "Repent!"), table turning and the declaration of "eat my flesh". As Wimber used to say, "God offends the mind to reveal the heart."

Besides, who made you the plumb line of divine style? There is actually a divine reason why God allows style to offend us: it is humbling.

FOUR: "They might have large numbers, but where's the depth?"

Said of growing churches with a big fringe. But wasn't this the atmosphere of Jesus' revolutionary campaigns in the dusty hills of Israel? It is true that the fringe grows bigger as a church grows, but having people along who are still only "thinking about" following Jesus is where we are supposed to be. Gays, drug addicts, people who are too busy for God, should be allowed to buzz around our churches – which, of course, gives it a very different feel to the small, committed, closeted church.

THREE: "It's alright for them!"

Aimed at leaders of larger churches, often in relation to what resources are available to them, compared to smaller churches. This conveniently forgets the fact that churches with more people also have more problems, bigger problems, and problems that cost more. Usually the challenges are multiplied exponentially. And for the leader, the bigger the church, the greater the stresses accompanying it. We probably would not enjoy being Brian Houston, even though it looks fun from a distance!

TWO: "We don't have the money or staff to do the 'excellence' thing."

Excellence is not just about the presentation of our venue and programmes. In fact, the highest and most impactful forms of excellence are completely free of charge. A smile. Warmth. Friendliness. Care. Thoughtfulness. There are many places that are excellent at presentation, but poor at warmth. Genuine joy and care for people will win out every time in the pursuit of souls for Christ. True excellence can be achieved for free!

And in at number 1...

ONE: "It's not about numbers."

Usually said by people with low numbers. They seem to miss the fact that God wrote a book called ... "Numbers" ... which was full of numbered lists. Because of God's love of numbers we know that Jesus had groups of 12, 72 and 120 disciples. He fed 5,000 people. 3,000 were saved on the Day of Pentecost. Each number represents a precious person, full of hopes, dreams, fears and purpose. Thankfully, for you, God even NUMBERS the hairs on your head. God is into LARGE numbers (currently about 7 billion). To miss that, is to miss His heart. Any church leader who is not into numbers will never have a large, growing, healthy church. Let's be honest, only insecure people say, "God isn't into numbers."

As one preacher put it, "If you count the offering, but not the people, it shows what you value most."

Epilogue:
Ready for Revival?

October 1996. I was flying from London on a flight that appeared to be stopping at every African village en route to Johannesburg. Sleeping through the night I was wakened by a startling vision of the glory of God. I lay terrified for several minutes, then slipped back into sleep. On arrival in South Africa the visions continued for several nights.

Whilst ministering in South Africa God began to move at a level I had seldom seen before. People were healed, saved, drug addicts overwhelmed by the power of God. There were sightings of angels, visions of the future, and whole congregations were taken up into wondrous meetings with God. Backsliders came back to Christ, the oppressed were delivered, the unsaved fell down, overcome by God's presence and got up saved! It was amazing. It was the fulfilment of a prophecy over my life and an answer to many prayers.

And yet, throughout this wondrous six weeks, I began to realise I felt desperately weak. God was moving in amazing power and seemed to be with me every second, but I was still in need. The same insecure, sinful, lonely, normal Jarrod. The same attitude, difficulties, pride and problems. Same old me, doing my best, living for God, making mistakes. I realised I could perform a miracle one minute and be an idiot the next. In fact, as the high's grew higher, the lows also stooped lower. I'd either be God's man of power for the hour, or a guilt-ridden wreck, desperately needing friendship and advice.

I had been praying for revival for many years, but this experience led me to question my expectations of revival. I believed, and still do, that amazing visitations of God are going to hit our nation in the next few decades.

But is revival an easy cure all, or a raging river that we must healthily learn to navigate?

God On Flesh

At the same time as ministering in South Africa, I was studying the life of Welsh revivalist, Evan Roberts. A man who saw amazing things happen in his ministry: thousands saved and healed, a nation impacted, and a fire spread throughout the globe. A man who we all should surely admire in some way.

Yet, as I studied, I realised here was a man with many emotional difficulties. A man with whom, at times, it was difficult to know whether he was being led by the Spirit of God or his own deep insecurities. A man who, by many accounts, had several nervous breakdowns that had him carried away from the very revival ministry he is hailed for.

I come from a spiritual heritage that infers that God would never harm us. If He tells us to do something, we'll always be okay. The experience of the Spirit will always be a good one.

This simplistic view of the spiritual realm was shattered for me when I met an African prophetess. All love and humility, but with unnerving accuracy, she told me all about myself and my family 6,000 miles away! Then, as I got to know her a little, she shared how the prophetic ministry almost cost her her marriage. That did not compute to me! Overwhelmed by visions and taken up with the spiritual realm, she said it was very easy to get unbalanced and unhealthy. She had to "control" how much she gave herself to spiritual experiences (1 Corinthians 14:32) and use some godly common sense regarding living as a spiritual person in a human world.

Scripturally, of course, people have had experiences of God that are painful and overwhelming. John fell terrified as though dead at the sight of Jesus; Daniel lay ill for ten days because of an overwhelming vision. Stephen was so taken up with God that he cried the very words that had him stoned to death (Acts 7:55)!

The concept that anything coming from God will only make us feel good and carries no risk is nonsense! When Almighty God touches human flesh, sometimes that touch is very gentle, but God can, and will, come in might, power, glory and overwhelming revelation. This is the glory that will visit the earth in the next few decades.

Some of us, due to our own lack of strength and character will become "ill" as Daniel did. Some, not because of God, but our own lack of "fitness" may die, unprepared for the glories that will engulf us. Some will find it too emotionally disturbing. Some will lose marriages, ministries and even their minds, because we do not understand the overwhelming nature of God.

Some churches will burst like brittle wineskins. Some leaders, who have developed an arrogant sense of entitlement, will be overtaken by youngsters coming through with fresh ideas from heaven and a humble hunger for His presence.

Many who have prayed for revival, have not prepared for revival.

Let us prepare.

My heart cry at the end of this little, hopefully inspiring, book, is *let us prepare!*

Let us be hungry for God and humble about our knowledge.

Let us reach out to connect and embrace each other.

Let men of the Word learn humbly from men of the Spirit about how to heighten the move of the Spirit in their lives.

Let men of the Spirit lose suspicion of skill and organisation and realise that Joseph and Daniel were as much revivalists as Ezekiel and Elijah. We must learn to build well if we are to retain the full harvest in the coming revival.

G. Campbell Morgan said, "Revival cannot be organised, but we can set our sails to catch the wind from heaven when God chooses to blow upon His people once again."

I believe that wind is blowing today.

Let's hoist the sails and adventure together!

Appendix I

The 1947 Smith Wigglesworth Prophecy in Full

"During the next few decades there will be two distinct moves of the Holy Spirit across the Church in Great Britain. The first move will affect every church that is open to receive it, and will be characterised by a restoration of the baptism and gifts of the Holy Spirit.

The second move of the Holy Spirit will result in people leaving historic churches and planting new churches.

In the duration of each of these moves, the people who are involved will say, 'This is a great revival.' But the Lord says, 'No, neither is this the great revival but both are steps towards it.'

When the new church phase is on the wane, there will be evidence in the churches of something that has not been seen before: a coming together of those with an emphasis on the Word and those with an emphasis on the Spirit. When the Word and the Spirit come together, there will be the biggest move of the Holy Spirit that the nation, and indeed, the world has ever seen. It will mark the beginning of a revival that will eclipse anything that has been witnessed within these shores, even the Wesleyan and Welsh revivals of former years. The outpouring of God's Spirit will flow over from the United Kingdom to mainland Europe, and from there, will begin a missionary move to the ends of the earth."

Appendix II
Church Health Checklists

The following is a compilation of Health Checklists from denominations around the world. It's amazing how similar so many are:

Eight Essential Qualities of Healthy Churches: Natural Church Development

1. Empowering leadership
2. Gift-oriented ministry development
3. Passionate spirituality
4. Functional structures
5. Inspiring worship services
6. Holistic small groups
7. Need-orientated evangelism
8. Loving relationships

Health Signs: Leith Anderson

1. Glorifying God
2. Producing disciples
3. Exercise of spiritual gifts

4. Relating positively to one's environment
5. Reproduction
6. Incorporation of newcomers
7. Openness to change
8. Trusting God and prayer

Ten Characteristics of a Healthy Church: Vision New England

1. God's empowering presence
2. God-exalting worship
3. Personal disciplines
4. Learning and growing in community
5. Commitment to loving/caring relationships
6. Servant-leadership development
7. An outward focus
8. Wise administration and accountability
9. Networking with the regional church
10. Stewardship and generosity

Characteristics of a Healthy Church: Willow Creek

1. Active spiritual formation
2. Authentic community (not public)
3. Contagious evangelism
4. Mobilised spiritual gifts
5. Good stewardship
6. Strong leadership
7. Cultural relevance
8. Effective generation-focused ministry
9. Collaboration and partnership

The Nine Habits of Highly Effective Churches: George Barna

1. They rely upon strategic leadership

2. They are organised to facilitate highly effective ministry

3. They emphasise developing significant relationships within the congregation

4. They invest themselves in genuine worship

5. They engage in strategic evangelism

6. They get their people involved in systematic theological growth

7. They utilise holistic stewardship practices

8. They serve the needy people in their community

9. They equip families to minister to themselves

Characteristics of a Healthy Church: Sonlife Ministries

1. Strong Christology

2. Clearly defined mission/purpose

3. Biblical strategy of a balanced win, build and equip

4. Regularly winning the lost

5. Strategically building the believers

6. On going equipping of the worker

7. Corporate and segment multiplication of shepherds

8. A broadly owned vision

9. A teachable spirit

Twelve Keys to an Effective Church: Kennon Callahan

1. Specific, concrete missional objectives

2. Pastoral and lay visitation

3. Corporate, dynamic worship

4. Significant relational groups

5. Strong leadership resources

6. Streamlined structure and solid, participatory decision making

7. Several competent programs and activities

8. Open accessibility
9. High visibility
10. Adequate parking, land and landscaping
11. Adequate space and facilities
12. Solid financial resources

Marks of Church Health: Bill Easum

1. Clear sense of mission
2. Authentic community
3. Indigenous worship
4. Lay mobilisation
5. Organic structure
6. Kingdom orientated
7. Experientially focused on Jesus Christ

Vital Signs of Healthy Churches: C. Peter Wagner

1. A positive pastor
2. A well-mobilised laity
3. Meeting members' needs
4. Proper balance of the dynamic relationship between celebration, congregation and cell
5. A common homogeneous denominator
6. Effective evangelistic methods
7. Biblical priorities

Windows into the 21st Century Church: Leadership Network

1. Effective leadership
2. Lay mobilisation
3. Cultural connectedness
4. Authentic community
5. Kingdom collaboration

Appendix II

[Compiled from various sources by Rowland Croucher from the Leadership Home Page of The Canadian Convention of Southern Baptists].

About Jarrod Cooper

Jarrod Cooper is an inspirer. Through teaching, song, worship and prophetic ministry he aims to inspire the Church to fullness in Jesus.

He leads Revive Church, a multi-site church meeting across Hull and East Yorkshire in the United Kingdom. He is an author, songwriter, conference speaker and broadcaster. His 30 minute TV and radio show, *Days of Wonder,* airs in several dozen nations many times a week.

Revive Church is devoted to **inspiring revival**, aiming to build and plant great God-filled churches and campuses. They also conduct revival events where God's glory moves, people are saved, leaders inspired and miracles abound!

In 2010 Jarrod launched the New Life Christian Academy, a school for 4-18 year olds in Hull devoted to raising extraordinary generations.

Jarrod is married to Victoria, is dad to Zach, and loves travelling, food, great coffee and the presence of God! Together they run Deep Blue Publishing which releases songs, albums and teaching products as they embark on missions around the world.

For further information, blog and resources visit:

www.JarrodCooper.net